Inspirational
Cross-Stitch

A wife of noble character, who can find?
. . . She selects wool and flax
and works with eager hands.
Proverbs 31: 10, 13

Inspirational
Cross-Stitch

by the Bucilla Design Group

Sterling Publishing Co., Inc. New York

A Sterling/Chapelle Book

For Bucilla

Robert P. Denise, President CEO

Glenn J. Nicholson, Executive V.P.

Jeffrey D. Steele, Executive V.P.

Designers: Joan Elliott,
Kooler Design Studio, Bonnie Smith,
and Maria Stanziani
Kooler Design Studio, Inc. Designers:
Linda Gillum, Nancy Rossi,
Barbara Baatz, and Sandy Orton

Bucilla ®
1 Oak Ridge Road
Hazelton, PA 18201-9764

For Chapelle

Owner: Jo Packham

Editors: Diane Kulkarni, Leslie Ridenour

Staff: Malissa Boatwright, Sara Casperson,
Rebecca Christensen, Amber Hansen,
Holly Hollingsworth, Susan Jorgensen, Susan Laws,
Amanda McPeck, Barbara Milburn, Pat Pearson,
Cindy Rooks, Cindy Stoeckl, Ryanne Webster, and
Nancy Whitley

Photographer: Kevin Dilley for Hazen Photography

Photo Stylist: Cherie Herrick

Watercolor Artist: Holly Fuller

Library of Congress Cataloging-in-Publication Data

Inspirational cross-stitch / by the Bucilla Design Group.
    p.   cm.
    "A Sterling/Chapelle book."
    Includes index.
    ISBN 0-8069-4279-7
    1. Cross-stitch--Patterns. 2. Christian art and symbolism.
I. Bucilla Design Group.
TT778.C76.I54 1996
746.44'3041--dc20
95-40527
CIP

3 5 7 9 10 8 6 4

A Sterling/Chapelle Book

First paperback edition published in **1997** by
Sterling Publishing Company, Inc.
387 Park Avenue South, New York, N.Y. 10016
© **1996** by Chapelle Limited
Distributed in Canada by Sterling Publishing
c/o Canadian Manda Group, One Atlantic Avenue, Suite **105**
Toronto, Ontario, Canada **M6K 3E7**
Distributed in Great Britain and Europe by Cassell PLC,
Wellington House, **125** Strand, London **WC2R 0BB**, England
Distributed in Australia by Capricorn Link (Australia) Pty Ltd.
P.O. Box **6651**, Baulkham Hills, Business Centre, NSW 2153, Australia
Printed in China
All rights reserved

Sterling **ISBN 0-8069-4279-7** Trade
0-8069-4280-0 Paper

If you have any questions or comments or would like information
on specialty products featured in this book, please contact:
Chapelle Ltd., Inc.
P. O. Box 9252
Ogden, Utah 84409
Phone: (801) 621-2777; FAX: (801) 621-2788

Scripture portions taken from the
HOLY BIBLE NEW INTERNATIONAL VERSION ©1973, 1978
by the International Bible Society

Contents

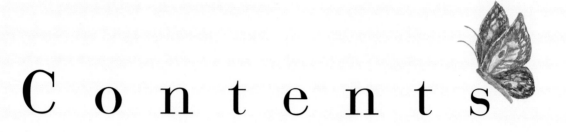

Love

Joy

C o n t e n t s

Peace

Patience

L
O
V
E

Where were you ...

while the morning stars
sang together
And all the angels
shouted for joy?

JOB 38:4,7

God is Love

Stitched on White Aida 18, design size is 3 ⁵/₈" by 5 ³/₈".
The fabric was cut 10" x 12".

Fabric	Design Size
Aida 11	6" x 8 ³/₄"
Aida 14	4 ³/₄" x 6 ⁷/₈"
Hardanger 22	3" x 4 ³/₈"

Anchor **DMC (used for sample)**

Step 1: Cross-stitch (2 strands)

50	+	605	Cranberry-vy. lt.
66	♥	3688	Mauve-med.
42	▫	3350	Dusty Rose-dk.
307	∨	977	Golden Brown-lt.
292	✿	3078	Golden Yellow-vy. lt.
265	✓	3348	Yellow Green-lt.
214	●	368	Pistachio Green-lt.
117	▲	341	Blue Violet-lt.
108	═	211	Lavender-lt.
119	✕	333	Blue Violet-dk.
380	I	839	Beige Brown-dk.
403	ß	310	Black

Step 2: Backstitch (1 strand)

42		3350	Dusty Rose-dk.
215		320	Pistachio Green-med.
119		333	Blue Violet-dk.
403		310	Black

Step 3: Straight Stitch (1 strand)

119		333	Blue Violet-dk.— center of flower
380		839	Beige Brown-dk.— butterflies

Top Stitch Count: 66 x 96

11

Noah's Ark

Stitched on White Aida **18**, design size is **4"** x **5 ³/₈"**.
The fabric was cut **10"** x **12"**.

Fabric	Design Size
Aida 11	6 ¹/₂" x 8 ⁷/₈"
Aida 14	5 ¹/₈" x 6 ⁷/₈"
Hardanger 22	3 ¹/₄" x 4 ³/₈"

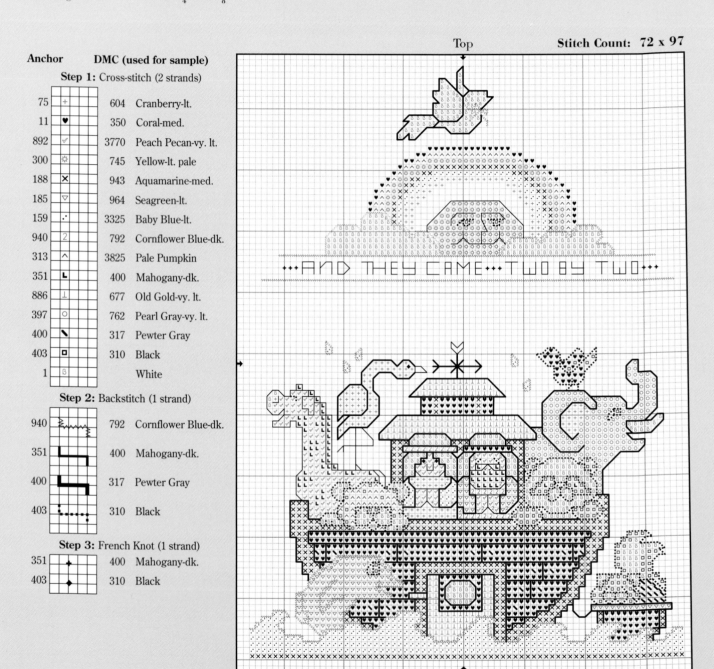

Top   Stitch Count: **72 x 97**

Anchor		DMC	(used for sample)

Step 1: Cross-stitch (2 strands)

75	+	604	Cranberry-lt.
11	♥	350	Coral-med.
892	⩗	3770	Peach Pecan-vy. lt.
300	✿	745	Yellow-lt. pale
188	✕	943	Aquamarine-med.
185	▽	964	Seagreen-lt.
159	··	3325	Baby Blue-lt.
940	2	792	Cornflower Blue-dk.
313	^	3825	Pale Pumpkin
351	L	400	Mahogany-dk.
886	⊥	677	Old Gold-vy. lt.
397	o	762	Pearl Gray-vy. lt.
400	◣	317	Pewter Gray
403	◻	310	Black
1	ß		White

Step 2: Backstitch (1 strand)

940	⌇	792	Cornflower Blue-dk.
351	⌐	400	Mahogany-dk.
400	⌐	317	Pewter Gray
403	····	310	Black

Step 3: French Knot (1 strand)

351	+	400	Mahogany-dk.
403	◆	310	Black

AND THEY CAME TWO BY TWO

Let Us Love One Another

Stitched on White Aida 14, the finished design size
is 5 ⁵/₈" x 3 ³/₄". The fabric was cut 12" x 10".

Fabric	Design Size
Aida 11	7 ¹/₈" x 4 ³/₄"
Aida 18	4 ³/₈" x 3"
Hardanger 22	3 ¹/₂" x 2 ³/₈"

Anchor		DMC (used for sample)	
Step 1: Cross-stitch (2 strands)			
24	^	776	Pink-med.
27	⌘	899	Rose-med.
8	/	761	Salmon-lt.
9	✦	760	Salmon
301	☼	744	Yellow-pale
214	⇑	368	Pistachio Green-lt.
215	✕	320	Pistachio Green-med.
160	=	813	Blue-lt.
130	▫	799	Delft-med.
95	♡	554	Violet-lt.
98	⋒	553	Violet-med.
Step 2: Backstitch (1 strand)			
215		320	Pistachio Green-med.
379		840	Beige Brown-med.
Step 3: Straight Stitch (1 strand)			
379		840	Beige Brown-med.
Step 4: French Knot (1 strand)			
24	●	776	Pink-med.
8	✖	761	Salmon-lt.
301	✶	744	Yellow-pale
215	●	320	Pistachio Green-med.
95	✦	554	Violet-lt.

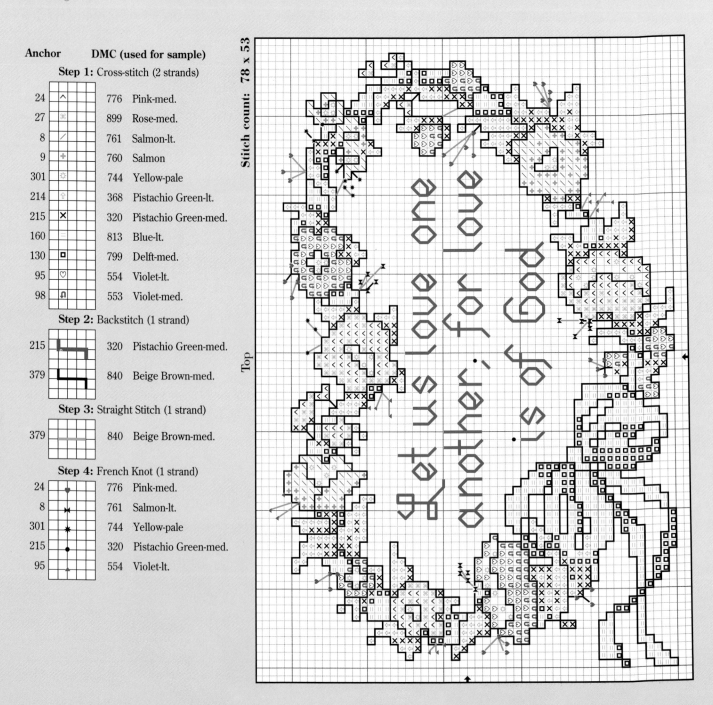

Stitch count: 78 x 53

Top

Bountiful Gifts

Stitched on White Aida 14, design size is
8 ¹/₈" x 11 ¹/₈". The fabric was cut 15" x 17".

Fabric	Design Size
Aida 11	10 ³/₈" x 14 ¹/₈"
Aida 18	6 ¹/₄" x 8 ⁵/₈"
Hardanger 22	5 ¹/₈" x 7"

Anchor   **DMC (used for sample)**

Step 1: Cross-stitch (2 strands)

Anchor		DMC	
40	∧	956	Geranium
13	♡	349	Coral-dk.
47	♥	321	Christmas Red
59	⌘	326	Rose-vy. dk.
316	═	970	Pumpkin-lt.
330	□	947	Burnt Orange
288	☼	445	Lemon-lt.
306	✚	725	Topaz
300	%	745	Yellow-lt. pale
301	⇧	744	Yellow-pale
307	⋈	977	Golden Brown-lt.
265	○	3348	Yellow Green-lt.
256	●	906	Parrot Green-med.
117	╱	341	Blue Violet-lt.
121	∩	794	Cornflower Blue-lt.
940	✕	792	Cornflower Blue-dk.

Step 2: Backstitch (1 strand)

Anchor		DMC	
59		326	Rose-vy. dk.
13		349	Coral-dk.
316		970	Pumpkin-lt.
330		947	Burnt Orange
307		977	Golden Brown-lt.
258		904	Parrot Green-vy. dk.
940		792	Cornflower Blue-dk.
940		792	Cornflower Blue-dk. (2 strands)

Step 3: French Knot (1 strand)

Anchor		DMC	
940	✶	792	Cornflower Blue-dk.

Optional Alphabet for Capital Letters

16

Top

Bottom

Token of Love Wedding Sampler

Stitched on Cream Aida 14, design size is 8 ⅝" x 11 ⅛". The fabric was cut 15" x 17".

Fabric	Design Size
Aida 11	10 ⅞" x 14 ⅛"
Aida 18	6 ⅝" x 8 ⅝"
Hardanger 22	5 ½" x 7 ⅛"

Anchor		DMC	(used for sample)

Step 1: Cross-stitch (2 strands)

Anchor		DMC	
48	\	818	Baby Pink
26	△	894	Carnation-vy. lt.
40	L	956	Geranium
11	◣	350	Coral-med.
50	○	3716	Wild Rose-lt.
22	✚	816	Garnet
880	▫	948	Peach-vy. lt.
4146	÷	754	Peach-lt.
8	♡	3824	Apricot-lt.
10	✳	352	Coral-lt.
316	∨	971	Pumpkin
292	#	3078	Golden Yellow-vy. lt.
295	✕	726	Topaz-lt.
298	‖	972	Canary-deep
265	%	3348	Yellow Green-lt.
243	⇩	988	Forest Green-med.
246	⋈	986	Forest Green-vy. dk.
158	◁	828	Blue-ultra vy. lt.
167	♣	3766	Peacock Blue-lt.
159	⏐	3325	Baby Blue-lt.
130	▲	799	Delft-med.
108	☐	211	Lavender-lt.
98	◢	553	Violet-med.
86	♥	3608	Plum-vy. lt.
349	♠	921	Copper
300	$	745	Yellow-lt. pale
890	▫	729	Old Gold-med.
901	♥	680	Old Gold-dk.
403	⊥	310	Black
1	◇		White

Step 2: Backstitch (1 strand)

Anchor		DMC	
349		921	Copper
400		414	Steel Gray-dk.

Step 3: Straight Stitch (1 strand)

1			White

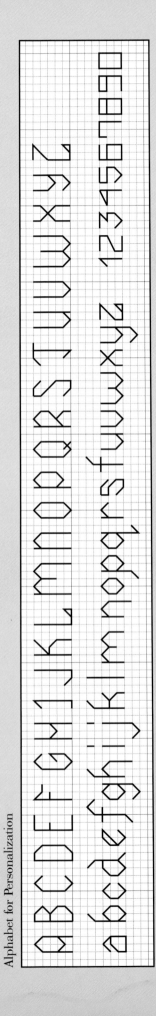

Alphabet for Personalization

Top

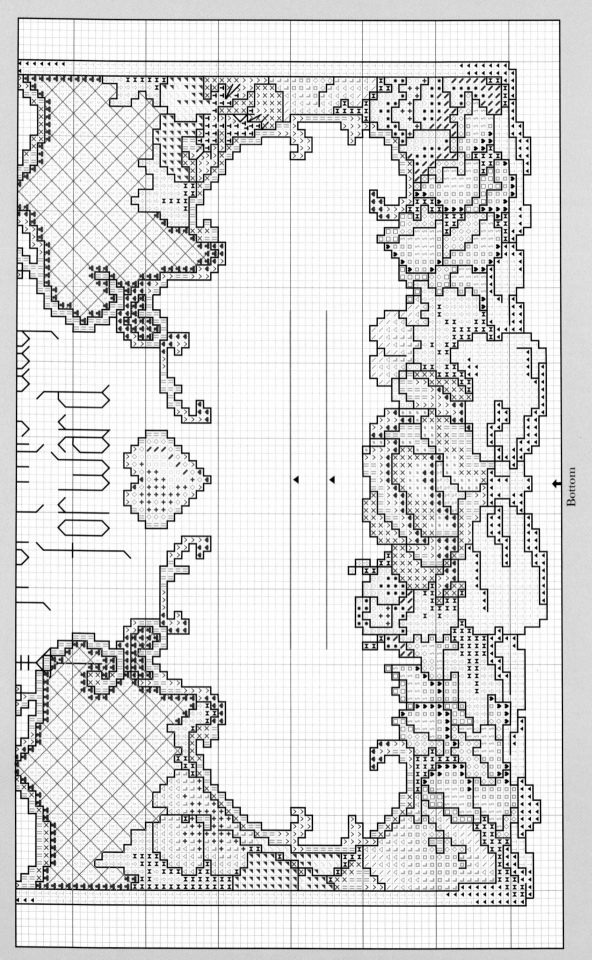

Bottom

Bless This Child

Stitched on White Aida **14**, design size is **10 $^3/_8$" x 12 $^7/_8$"**. The fabric was cut **17" x 19"**.

Fabric	Design Size
Aida **11**	13 $^1/_8$" x 16 $^1/_2$"
Aida **18**	8 $^1/_8$" x 10"
Hardanger **22**	6 $^5/_8$" x 8 $^1/_4$"

Anchor   **DMC (used for sample)**

Step 1: Cross-stitch (2 strands)

Anchor		DMC	
48	+	818	Baby Pink
25	2	3326	Rose-lt.
42	♥	335	Rose
323	⇩	722	Orange Spice-lt.
300	#	745	Yellow-lt. pale
301	∴	744	Yellow-pale
203	✓	564	Jade-vy. lt.
204	◆	912	Emerald Green-lt.
185	△	964	Seagreen-lt.
186	▢	959	Seagreen-med.
158	©	775	Baby Blue-vy. lt.
160	✕	813	Blue-lt.
130	✳	799	Delft-med.
108	=	211	Lavender-lt.
105	●	209	Lavender-dk.
85	$	3609	Plum-ultra lt.
87	⌘	3607	Plum-lt.
370	❨	434	Brown-lt.
886	⊥	677	Old Gold-vy. lt.
397	S	762	Pearl Gray-vy. lt.
399	8	452	Shell Gray-med.
236	⋈	3799	Pewter Gray-vy. dk.
366	☆	951	Peach Pecan-lt.
1	W		White

Step 2: Backstitch (1 strand)

Anchor		DMC	
42		335	Rose
323		722	Orange Spice-lt. (2 strands)
130		799	Delft-med.
316		970	Pumpkin-lt.
400		317	Pewter Gray
236		3799	Pewter Gray-vy. dk.

Top Left

Stitch count: 145 x 181

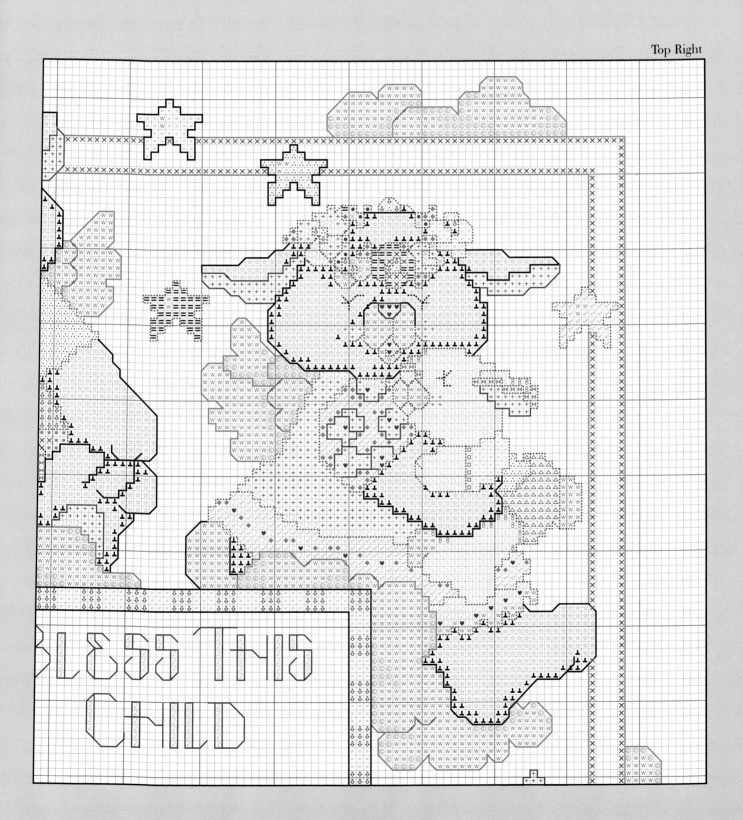

Alphabet for Personalization

ABCDEFGHIJKLM
NOPQRSTUVWXYZ

0123456789

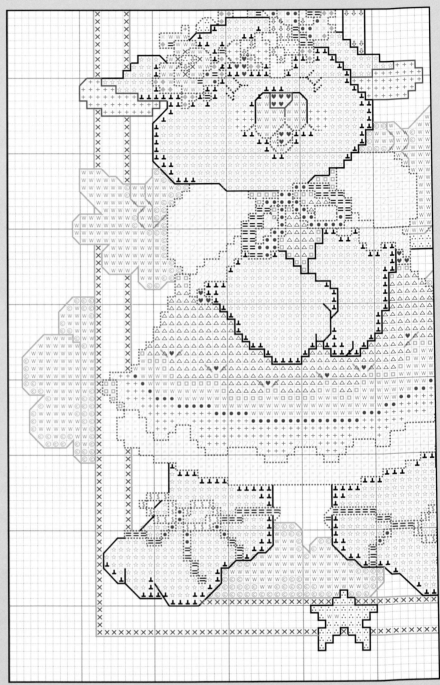

Bottom Left

26

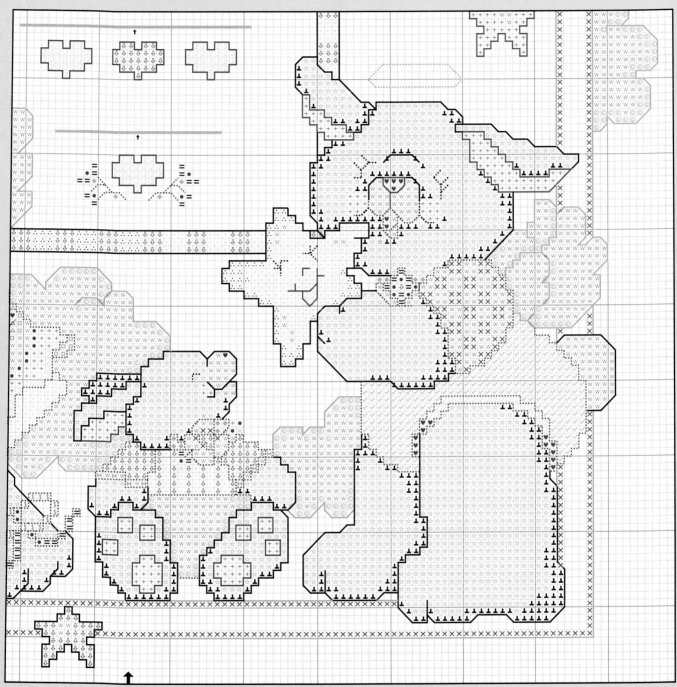

Bottom Right

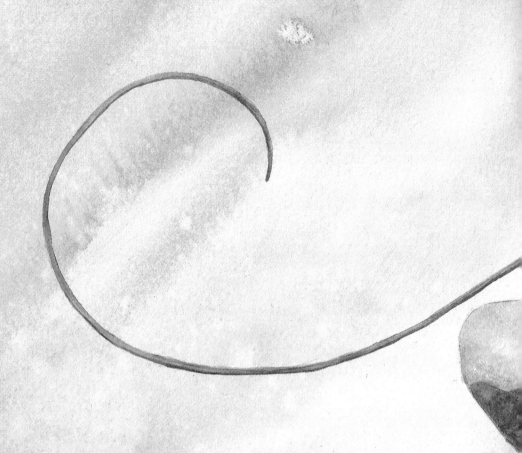

*We haven't yet got eyes that can gaze
into all the splendour that God has created,
but we shall get them one day,
and that will be the finest fairy tale of all,
for we shall be in it ourselves.*

HANS CHRISTIAN ANDERSON

JOY

Jesus at the Door

Stitched on White Aida 14, the finished design size is 9 $\frac{5}{8}$" x 11 $\frac{1}{2}$". The fabric was cut 16" x 18". An optional verse is provided to accompany piece.

Fabric

Aida 11

Aida 18

Hardanger 22

Design Size

12 $\frac{1}{4}$" x 14 $\frac{5}{8}$"

7 $\frac{1}{2}$" x 9"

6 $\frac{1}{8}$" x 7 $\frac{3}{8}$"

Anchor **DMC (used for sample)**

Step 1: Cross-stitch (2 strands)

Anchor		DMC	
35	✛	3801	Light Christmas Red
50	♥	3706	Melon-med.
72	ß	902	Garnet-vy. dk.
891	☆	676	Old Gold-lt.
206	∴	955	Nile Green-lt.
210	+	562	Jade-med.
879	□	890	Pistachio Green-ultra dk.
257	2	3346	Hunter Green
158		775	Baby Blue-vy. lt.
920	◇	932	Antique Blue-lt.
921	⌘	931	Antique Blue-med.
149	＼	311	Navy Blue-med.
108	⋈	211	Lavender-lt.
870	◩	3042	Antique Violet-lt.
387	×	712	Cream
4146	↰	754	Peach-lt.
5975	▲	356	Terra Cotta-med.
914	%	3064	Pecan-lt.
371		433	Brown-med.
382	#	3371	Black Brown
1	W		White
900	●	648	Beaver Gray-lt.
399	∨	318	Steel Gray-lt.
403	ı	310	Black

Step 2: Backstitch (1 strand)

382		3371	Black Brown
403		310	Black

Step 3: Couching Stitch

399		318	Steel Gray-lt. (2 strands)
403		310	Black (6 strands)

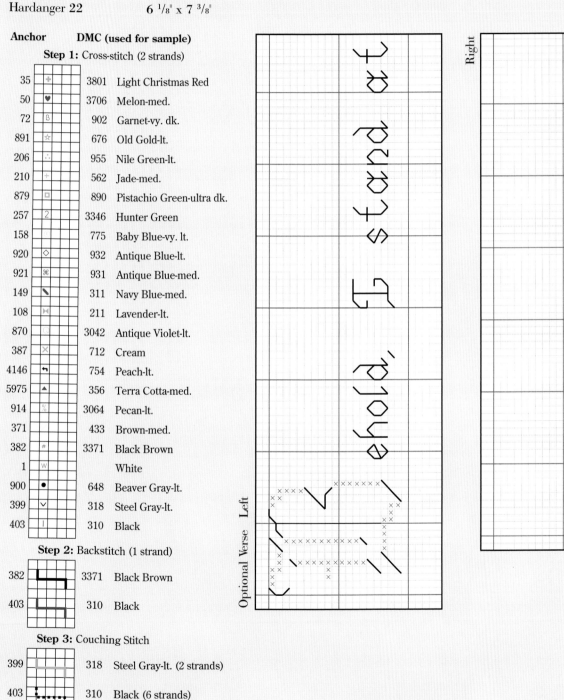

Optional Verse   Left   Right

Behold, I stand at the door, and knock. Rev. 3:20

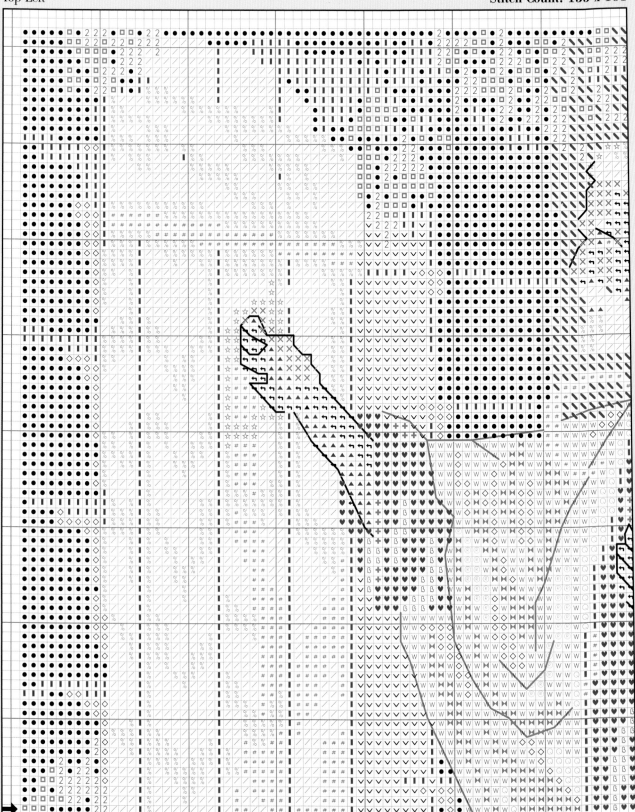

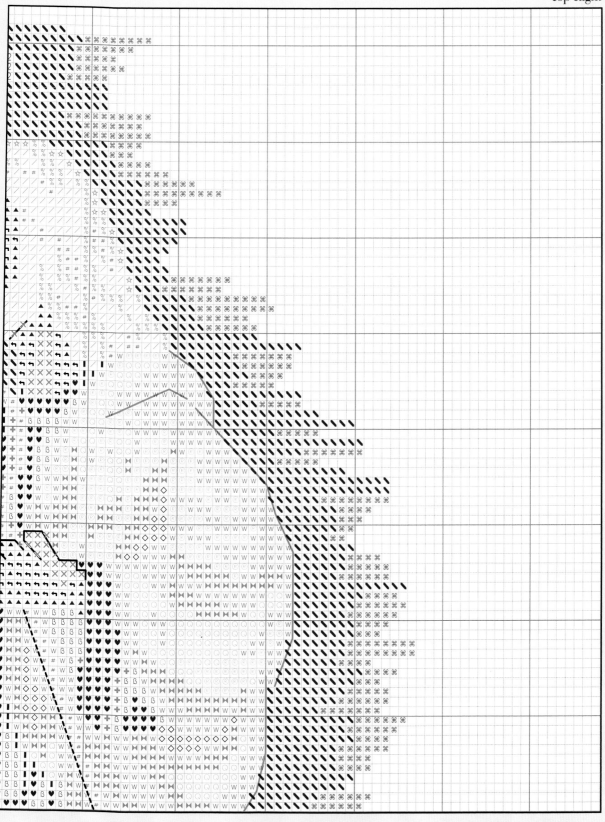

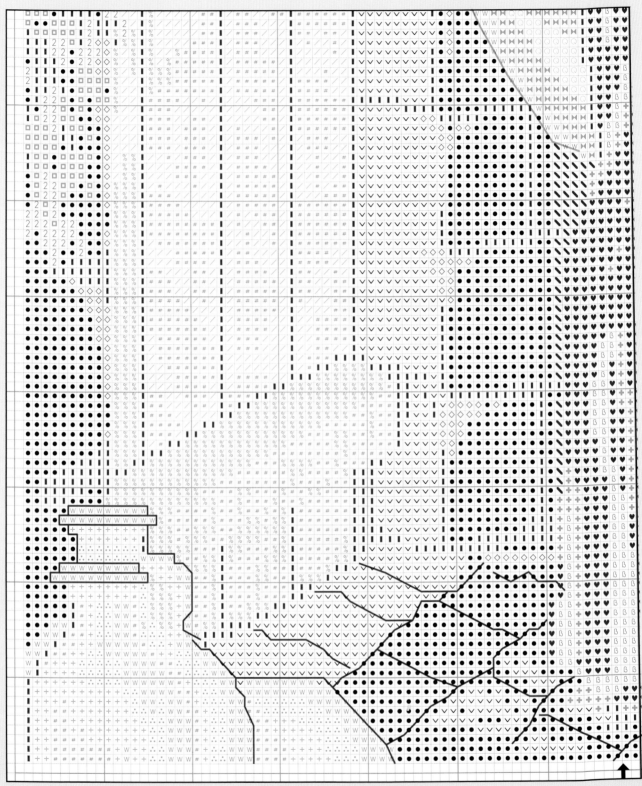

Bottom Left

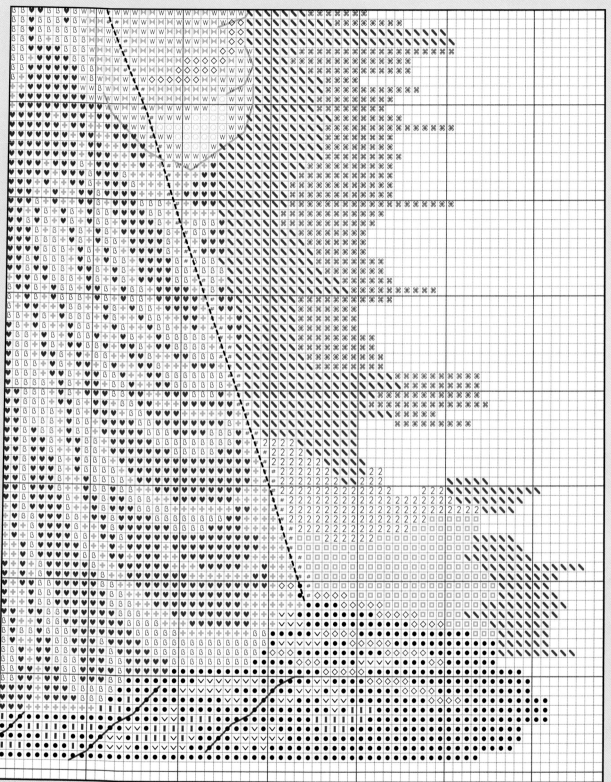

Bottom Right

Joy to the World

Stitched on Ivory Aida 14, the finished design size is 10 ³/₈" x 15 ⁵/₈". The fabric was cut 17" x 22". You will need to purchase ¹/₂ yd. of seasonal fabric and matching thread to finish your stocking. For lining: ¹/₂ yd. of matching fabric and quilt batting. See page 40 for finishing instructions.

Fabric	Design Size
Aida 11	13 ¹/₄" x 19 ⁷/₈"
Aida 18	8 ¹/₈" x 12 ¹/₈"
Hardanger 22	6 ⁵/₈" x 10"

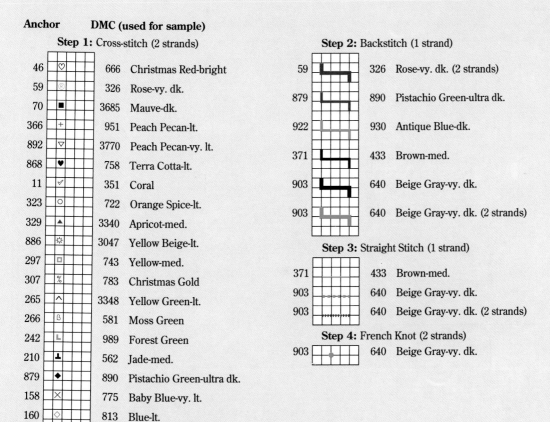

Anchor   **DMC (used for sample)**

Step 1: Cross-stitch (2 strands)

Anchor		DMC	
46	♡	666	Christmas Red-bright
59	⊙	326	Rose-vy. dk.
70	■	3685	Mauve-dk.
366	+	951	Peach Pecan-lt.
892	▽	3770	Peach Pecan-vy. lt.
868	♥	758	Terra Cotta-lt.
11	✓	351	Coral
323	○	722	Orange Spice-lt.
329	▲	3340	Apricot-med.
886	☼	3047	Yellow Beige-lt.
297	□	743	Yellow-med.
307	%	783	Christmas Gold
265	^	3348	Yellow Green-lt.
266	ß	581	Moss Green
242	L	989	Forest Green
210	⊥	562	Jade-med.
879	◆	890	Pistachio Green-ultra dk.
158	✕	775	Baby Blue-vy. lt.
160	◇	813	Blue-lt.
978	▼	322	Navy Blue-vy. lt.
922	⋈	930	Antique Blue-dk.
117	=	341	Blue Violet-lt.
118	∨	340	Blue Violet-med.
119	⌘	333	Blue Violet-dk.
370	✳	434	Brown-lt.
357	Ω	801	Coffee Brown-dk.
903	T	640	Beige Gray-vy. dk.
1			White
5975	☆	⟋ 356	Terra Cotta-med.
868		⟍ 758	Terra Cotta-lt.
371	⟋	⟋ 433	Brown-med.
5975		⟍ 356	Terra Cotta-med.

Step 2: Backstitch (1 strand)

Anchor		DMC	
59		326	Rose-vy. dk. (2 strands)
879		890	Pistachio Green-ultra dk.
922		930	Antique Blue-dk.
371		433	Brown-med.
903		640	Beige Gray-vy. dk.
903		640	Beige Gray-vy. dk. (2 strands)

Step 3: Straight Stitch (1 strand)

Anchor		DMC	
371		433	Brown-med.
903		640	Beige Gray-vy. dk.
903		640	Beige Gray-vy. dk. (2 strands)

Step 4: French Knot (2 strands)

Anchor		DMC	
903		640	Beige Gray-vy. dk.

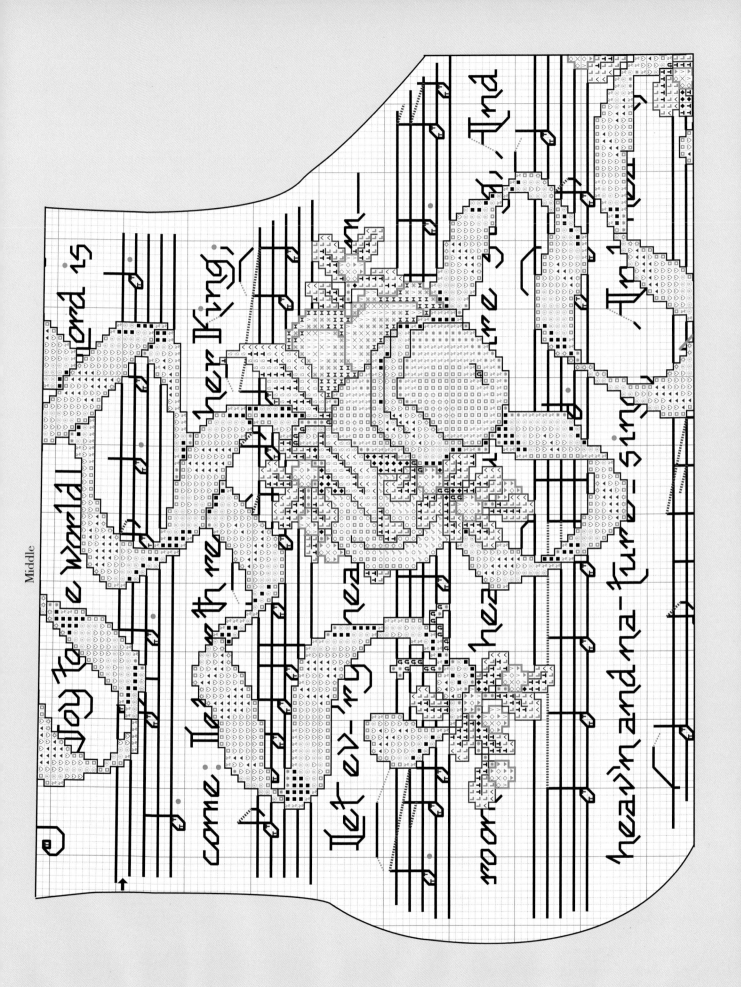

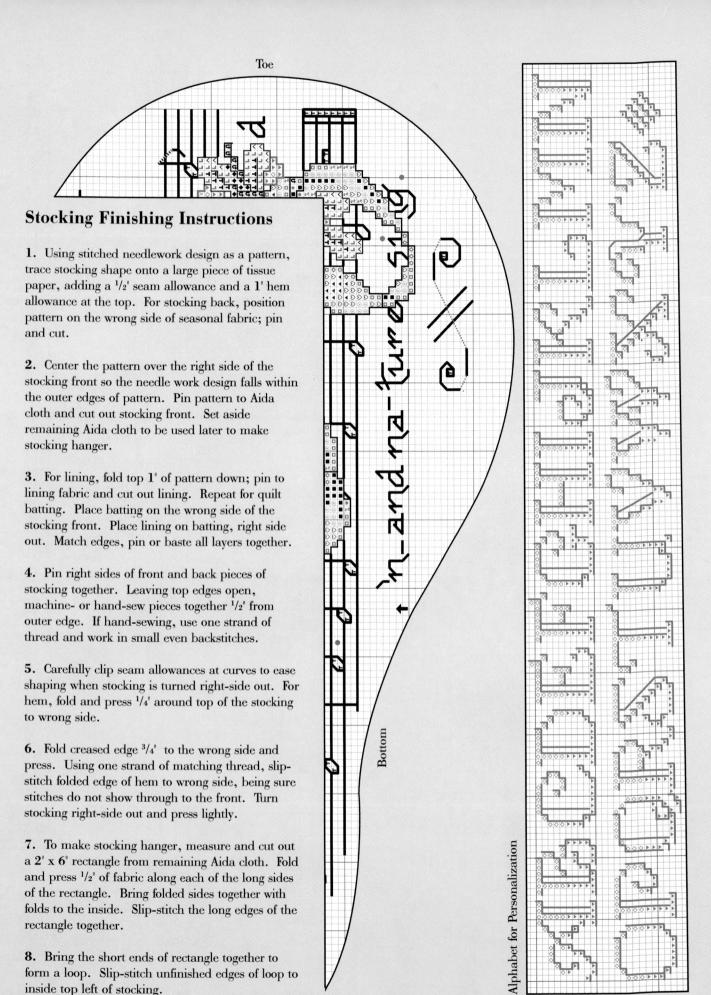

Stocking Finishing Instructions

1. Using stitched needlework design as a pattern, trace stocking shape onto a large piece of tissue paper, adding a ¹/₂" seam allowance and a 1" hem allowance at the top. For stocking back, position pattern on the wrong side of seasonal fabric; pin and cut.

2. Center the pattern over the right side of the stocking front so the needle work design falls within the outer edges of pattern. Pin pattern to Aida cloth and cut out stocking front. Set aside remaining Aida cloth to be used later to make stocking hanger.

3. For lining, fold top 1" of pattern down; pin to lining fabric and cut out lining. Repeat for quilt batting. Place batting on the wrong side of the stocking front. Place lining on batting, right side out. Match edges, pin or baste all layers together.

4. Pin right sides of front and back pieces of stocking together. Leaving top edges open, machine- or hand-sew pieces together ¹/₂" from outer edge. If hand-sewing, use one strand of thread and work in small even backstitches.

5. Carefully clip seam allowances at curves to ease shaping when stocking is turned right-side out. For hem, fold and press ¹/₄" around top of the stocking to wrong side.

6. Fold creased edge ³/₄" to the wrong side and press. Using one strand of matching thread, slip-stitch folded edge of hem to wrong side, being sure stitches do not show through to the front. Turn stocking right-side out and press lightly.

7. To make stocking hanger, measure and cut out a 2" x 6" rectangle from remaining Aida cloth. Fold and press ¹/₂" of fabric along each of the long sides of the rectangle. Bring folded sides together with folds to the inside. Slip-stitch the long edges of the rectangle together.

8. Bring the short ends of rectangle together to form a loop. Slip-stitch unfinished edges of loop to inside top left of stocking.

Toe

Bottom

Alphabet for Personalization

Hark! The Herald Angels

Stitched on White Aida **14**, the finished design size is 9 ⁷/₈" x 16". The fabric was cut **16" x 22"**. You will need to purchase ½ yd. of seasonal fabric and matching thread to finish your stocking. For lining: ½ yd. of matching fabric and quilt batting. See page 40 for finishing instructions.

Fabric	Design Size
Aida **11**	12 ⁵/₈" x 20 ¼"
Aida **18**	7 ³/₄" x 12 ³/₈"
Hardanger **22**	6 ³/₈" x 10 ⅛"

Anchor		DMC (used for sample)	

Step 1: Cross-stitch (2 strands)

Anchor		DMC	
24	+	776	Pink-med.
76	⌘	962	Wild Rose-med.
46	♥	666	Christmas Red-bright
59	■	326	Rose-vy. dk.
880	♡	948	Peach-vy. lt.
4146	✕	754	Peach-lt.
292	☆	3078	Golden Yellow-vy. lt.
295	✳	726	Topaz-lt.
890	^	729	Old Gold-med.
203	L	954	Nile Green
204	▽	912	Emerald Green-lt.
923	◣	699	Christmas Green
159	◇	3325	Baby Blue-lt.
130	ß	799	Delft-med.
132	⋈	797	Royal Blue
347	T	402	Mahogany-vy. lt.
370	▣	434	Brown-lt.
371	⩍	433	Brown-med.
397	✓	3072	Beaver Gray-vy. lt.
1	?		White

Step 2: Backstitch (1 strand)

Anchor		DMC	
59		326	Rose-vy. dk.
295		726	Topaz-lt. (2 strands)
923		699	Christmas Green
130		799	Delft-med.
132		797	Royal Blue
371		433	Brown-med.
371		433	Brown-med. (2 strands)
400		414	Steel Gray-dk. (2 strands)

Step 3: French Knot (2 strands)

Anchor		DMC	
371	●	433	Brown-med.
400	●	414	Steel Gray-dk.

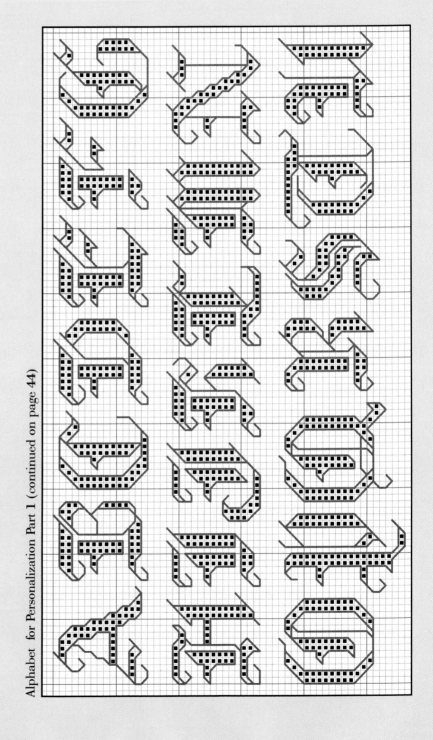

Alphabet for Personalization Part 1 (continued on page 44)

Top

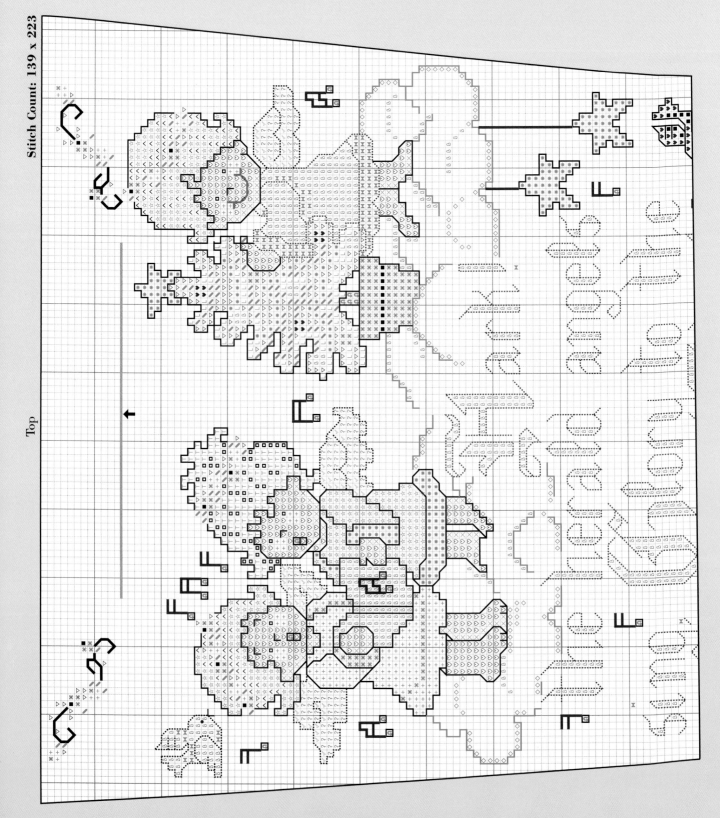

Middle

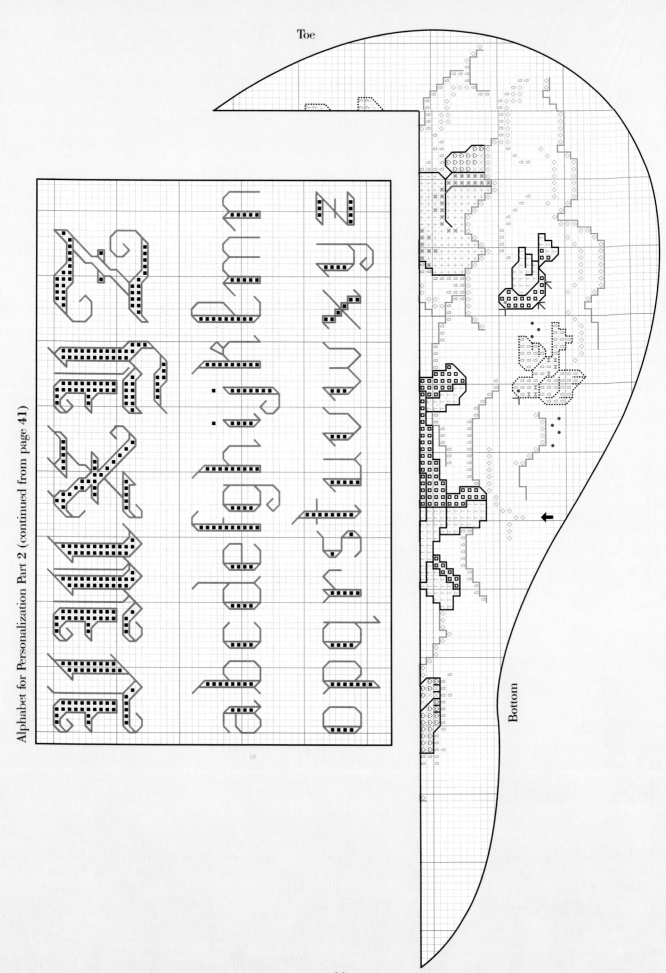

Toe

Alphabet for Personalization Part 2 (continued from page 41)

Bottom

Nativity

Stitched on Cream Aida 14, the finished design
size is 14" x 8 5/8". The fabric was cut 20" x 15".

Fabric   **Design Size**
Aida 11   17 7/8" x 10 7/8"
Aida 18   10 7/8" x 6 5/8"
Hardanger 22   8 7/8" x 5 1/2"

Anchor   **DMC (used for sample)**

Step 1: Cross-stitch (2 strands)

Anchor		DMC	
892		819	Baby Pink-lt.
25	#	3326	Rose-lt.
892	ß	3770	Peach Pecan-vy. lt.
868	÷	758	Terra Cotta-lt.
387	$	712	Cream
886	%	677	Old Gold-vy. lt.
297	&	743	Yellow-med.
891	←	676	Old Gold-lt.
307	▼	783	Christmas Gold
264	ç	772	Pine Green-lt.
256	?	704	Chartreuse-bright
185	>	964	Seagreen-lt.
186	✓	959	Seagreen-med.
158	⌘	3756	Baby Blue-ultra vy. lt.
158	£	775	Baby Blue-vy. lt.
160	/	813	Blue-lt.
85	^	3609	Plum-ultra lt.
869	□	3743	Antique Violet-vy. lt.
104	▲	210	Lavender-med.
313	＼	3825	Pale Pumpkin

Anchor		DMC	
324	+	922	Copper-lt.
933	⇩	543	Beige Brown-ultra vy. lt.
379	⊥	840	Beige Brown-med.
380	✳	839	Beige Brown-dk.
370	◆	434	Brown-lt.
397	◇	3072	Beaver Gray-vy. lt.
398	★	415	Pearl Gray
1	¢		White

Step 2: Backstitch (1 strand)

Anchor		DMC	
978		322	Navy Blue-vy. lt.
324		922	Copper-lt.
370		434	Brown-lt.
399		318	Steel Gray-lt.

Step 3: French Knot (1 strand)

Anchor		DMC	
978		322	Navy Blue-vy. lt.
324	◆	922	Copper-lt.

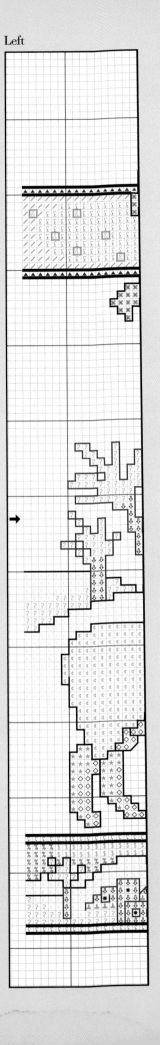

Left

46

ehold, I bring you good tid

ngs of great joy

Bless My Kitchen

Stitched on White Aida 14, the finished design is 11 $\frac{1}{8}$" x 8 $\frac{1}{8}$". The fabric was cut 17" x 14".

Fabric	Design Size
Aida 11	14 $\frac{1}{8}$" x 10 $\frac{3}{8}$"
Aida 18	8 $\frac{5}{8}$" x 6 $\frac{3}{8}$"
Hardanger 22	7 $\frac{1}{8}$" x 5 $\frac{1}{8}$"

Anchor		DMC (used for sample)	
Step 1: Cross-stitch (2 strands)			
892	○	819	Baby Pink-lt.
24	△	776	Pink-med.
76	♥	962	Wild Rose-med.
880	⇩	948	Peach-vy. lt.
8	▫	353	Peach
11	⋈	351	Coral
297	‖	743	Yellow-med.
203	✕	564	Jade-vy. lt.
206	+	955	Nile Green-lt.
209	♡	913	Nile Green-med.
212	◣	561	Jade-vy. dk.
158	∨	775	Baby Blue-vy. lt.
159	∟	3325	Baby Blue-lt.
978	✳	322	Navy Blue-vy. lt.
104	◇	210	Lavender-med.
110	✦	208	Lavender-vy. dk.
387	╲	822	Beige Gray-lt.
309	⊤	435	Brown-vy. lt.
352	♣	300	Mahogany-vy. dk.

Step 2: Backstitch (1 strand)			
978		322	Navy Blue-vy. lt. (2 strands)
352		300	Mahogany-vy. dk.
352		300	Mahogany-vy. dk. (2 strands)
399		318	Steel Gray-lt.

Step 3: French Knot (3 strands)			
978	■	322	Navy Blue-vy. lt.
352		300	Mahogany-vy. dk.

Alternate Verse

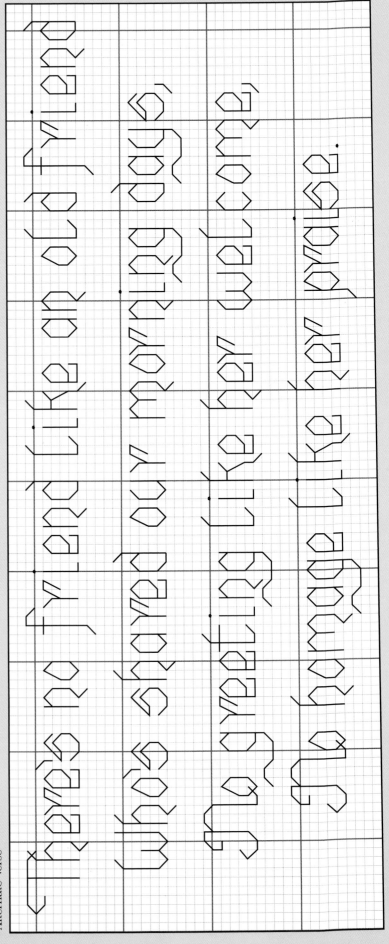

Bless my little
And those w
May they find son
and happines

A Friend Loveth at All Times

Stitched on White Aida 14, the finished design size is
4 ¹/₈" x 6". The fabric was cut 10" x 12". See photo on
page 5.

Fabric	Design Size
Aida 11	5 ¹/₈" x 7 ⁵/₈"
Aida 18	3 ¹/₈" x 4 ⁵/₈"
Hardanger 22	2 ⁵/₈" x 3 ⁷/₈"

Stitch Count: 57 x 84

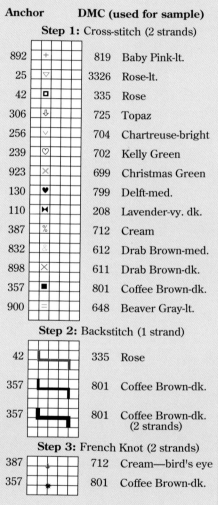

Anchor		DMC (used for sample)	
Step 1: Cross-stitch (2 strands)			
892	+	819	Baby Pink-lt.
25	▽	3326	Rose-lt.
42	◻	335	Rose
306	⇩	725	Topaz
256	∨	704	Chartreuse-bright
239	♡	702	Kelly Green
923	✕	699	Christmas Green
130	♥	799	Delft-med.
110	⋈	208	Lavender-vy. dk.
387	%	712	Cream
832	&	612	Drab Brown-med.
898	✕	611	Drab Brown-dk.
357	■	801	Coffee Brown-dk.
900	=	648	Beaver Gray-lt.

Step 2: Backstitch (1 strand)			
42		335	Rose
357		801	Coffee Brown-dk.
357		801	Coffee Brown-dk. (2 strands)

Step 3: French Knot (2 strands)			
387		712	Cream—bird's eye
357		801	Coffee Brown-dk.

Blessed Are You

Stitched on Ivory Aida 14, the finished design size
is 11" x 14 ¹/₈". The fabric was cut 17" x 20".

Fabric	Design Size
Aida 11	14" x 17 ⁷/₈"
Aida 18	8 ¹/₂" x 11"
Hardanger 22	7" x 9"

Alternate Verse

Anchor   DMC (used for sample)

Step 1: Cross-stitch (2 strands)

Anchor		DMC	
76	+	603	Cranberry
59	♡	600	Cranberry-vy. dk.
70	◆	3685	Mauve-dk.
316	○	740	Tangerine
293	☼	727	Topaz-vy. lt.
303	∨	742	Tangerine-lt.
255	/	907	Parrot Green-lt.
203	✕	564	Jade-vy. lt.
213	¥	369	Pistachio Green-vy. lt.
214	2	368	Pistachio Green-lt.
265	^	3348	Yellow Green-lt.
266	‖	581	Moss Green
117	⌘	341	Blue Violet-lt.
121	⇩	793	Cornflower Blue-med.
162	3	517	Wedgewood-dk.
108	△	211	Lavender-lt.
98	◣	553	Violet-med.
119	▮	333	Blue Violet-dk.
347	F	402	Mahogany-vy. lt.
349	⊥	301	Mahogany-med.
887	%	422	Hazel Nut Brown-lt.
380	B	839	Beige Brown-dk.
357	◨	801	Coffee Brown-dk.
900	∨	928	Slate Green-lt.
400	◿	414	Steel Gray-dk.
236	8	3799	Pewter Gray-vy. dk.
403	♠	310	Black
1	W		White

Step 2: Half Cross-stitch (2 strands)

Anchor		DMC	
887	A	422	Hazel Nut Brown-lt.
373	S	3045	Yellow Beige-dk.

Step 3: Backstitch (1 strand)

Anchor		DMC	
121		793	Cornflower Blue-med.
162		517	Wedgewood-dk.
380		839	Beige Brown-dk.
357		801	Coffee Brown-dk.
403		310	Black

Step 4: Couching Stitch (3 strands)

Anchor		DMC	
265		3348	Yellow Green-lt.

Step 5: French Knot (1 strand)

Anchor		DMC	
162	•	517	Wedgewood-dk. (2 strands)
1	•		White

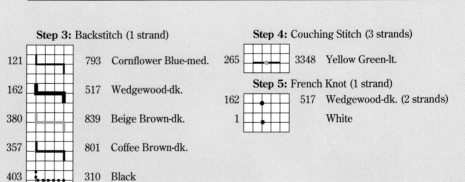

Nature is painting
For us, day after day,
Pictures of infinite
Beauty if only we
Have the eyes to
See them.

John Ruskin

Bottom Left

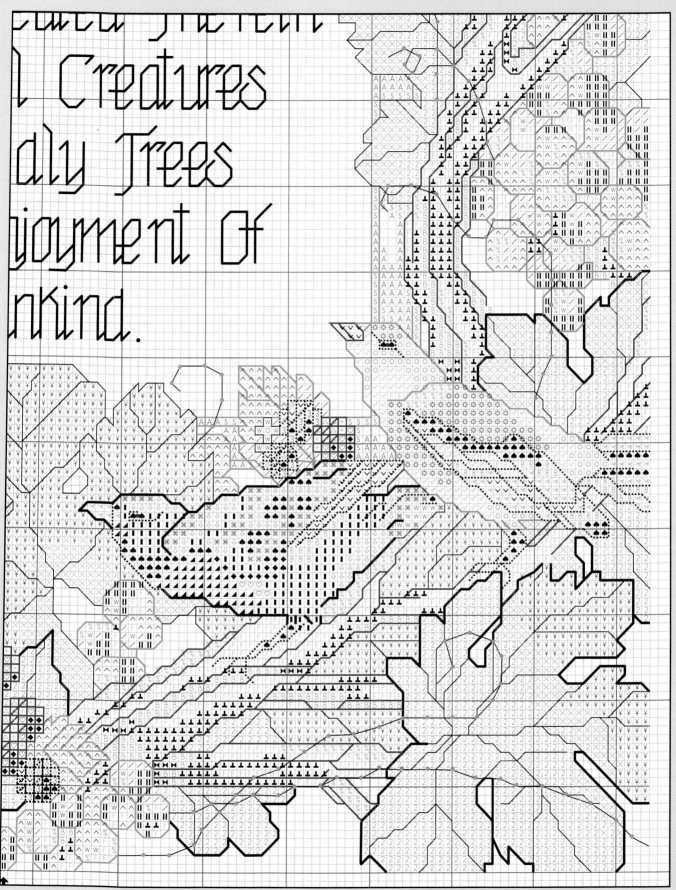

Creatures

lly Trees

yoyment Of

nkind.

Psalm 100

Stitched on Ivory Aida 14, the finished design size is 10 $\frac{3}{4}$" x 13 $\frac{5}{8}$". The fabric was cut 17" x 20".

Fabric	Design Size
Aida 11	13 $\frac{3}{4}$" x 17 $\frac{3}{8}$"
Aida 18	8 $\frac{3}{8}$" x 10 $\frac{5}{8}$"
Hardanger 22	6 $\frac{7}{8}$" x 8 $\frac{5}{8}$"

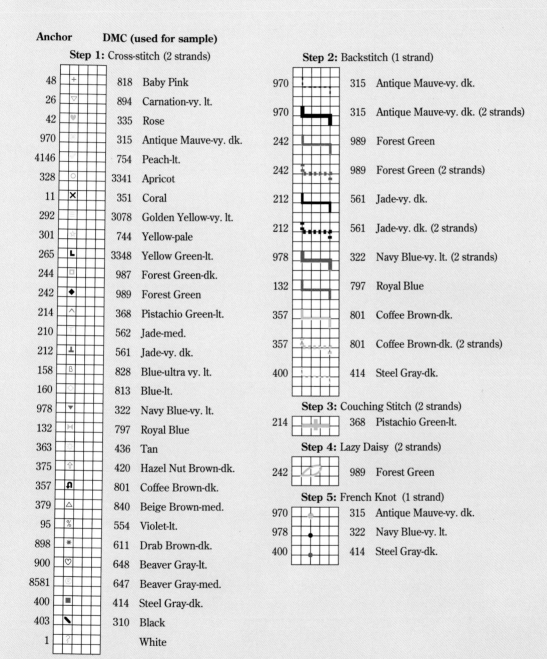

Anchor   **DMC (used for sample)**

Step 1: Cross-stitch (2 strands)

Anchor		DMC	
48	+	818	Baby Pink
26	▽	894	Carnation-vy. lt.
42	♥	335	Rose
970		315	Antique Mauve-vy. dk.
4146		754	Peach-lt.
328	○	3341	Apricot
11	✕	351	Coral
292	=	3078	Golden Yellow-vy. lt.
301	☆	744	Yellow-pale
265	L	3348	Yellow Green-lt.
244	□	987	Forest Green-dk.
242	◆	989	Forest Green
214	∧	368	Pistachio Green-lt.
210		562	Jade-med.
212	⊥	561	Jade-vy. dk.
158	ß	828	Blue-ultra vy. lt.
160	◇	813	Blue-lt.
978	▼	322	Navy Blue-vy. lt.
132	⋈	797	Royal Blue
363		436	Tan
375	⇧	420	Hazel Nut Brown-dk.
357	∩	801	Coffee Brown-dk.
379	△	840	Beige Brown-med.
95	%	554	Violet-lt.
898	✳	611	Drab Brown-dk.
900	♡	648	Beaver Gray-lt.
8581		647	Beaver Gray-med.
400	■	414	Steel Gray-dk.
403	◥	310	Black
1	?		White

Step 2: Backstitch (1 strand)

Anchor		DMC	
970		315	Antique Mauve-vy. dk.
970		315	Antique Mauve-vy. dk. (2 strands)
242		989	Forest Green
242		989	Forest Green (2 strands)
212		561	Jade-vy. dk.
212		561	Jade-vy. dk. (2 strands)
978		322	Navy Blue-vy. lt. (2 strands)
132		797	Royal Blue
357		801	Coffee Brown-dk.
357		801	Coffee Brown-dk. (2 strands)
400		414	Steel Gray-dk.

Step 3: Couching Stitch (2 strands)

Anchor		DMC	
214		368	Pistachio Green-lt.

Step 4: Lazy Daisy (2 strands)

Anchor		DMC	
242		989	Forest Green

Step 5: French Knot (1 strand)

Anchor		DMC	
970		315	Antique Mauve-vy. dk.
978		322	Navy Blue-vy. lt.
400		414	Steel Gray-dk.

ful noise unto
all ye lands,
with gladness:
his presence
nging.

nter int[o]
with the
and into his cou[rt]
be thankful u[nto]
bless his

1Psa
100:1

Bottom Left

o his gates

anksgiving,

rts with praise:

nto him, and

s name.

dm

246

"Just living is not enough,"
said the butterfly.
"One must have sunshine,
freedom,
and little flowers!"

HANS CHRISTIAN ANDERSON

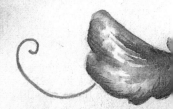

Blessed are the peacemakers, for they shall be called the children of God.

MATTHEW 5:9

Blessed Are the Peacemakers

Stitched on White Aida 14, the finished design size is 6" x 4 ¼". The fabric was cut 12" x 10".

Fabrics	Design Size
Aida 11	7 ⁵⁄₈" x 5 ³⁄₈"
Aida 18	4 ⁵⁄₈" x 3 ¼"
Hardanger 22	3 ⁷⁄₈" x 2 ⁵⁄₈"

Anchor		DMC (used for sample)	
Step 1: Cross-stitch (2 strands)			
26	○	894	Carnation-vy. lt.
40	▫	956	Geranium
59	♥	600	Cranberry-vy. dk.
297	△	743	Yellow-med.
298	♣	972	Canary-deep
256	+	704	Chartreuse-bright
239	×	702	Kelly Green
923	◄	699	Christmas Green
159	^	3325	Baby Blue-lt.
978	♦	322	Navy Blue-vy. lt.
95	⇧	554	Violet-lt.
105	⊥	209	Lavender-dk.
110	✳	208	Lavender-vy. dk.

Step 2: Backstitch (1 strand)			
59		600	Cranberry-vy. dk.
923		699	Christmas Green (2 strands)
978		322	Navy Blue-vy. lt.
978		322	Navy Blue-vy. lt. (2 strands)
110		208	Lavender-vy. dk.

Step 3: French Knot (2 strands)			
978	▲	322	Navy Blue-vy. lt.

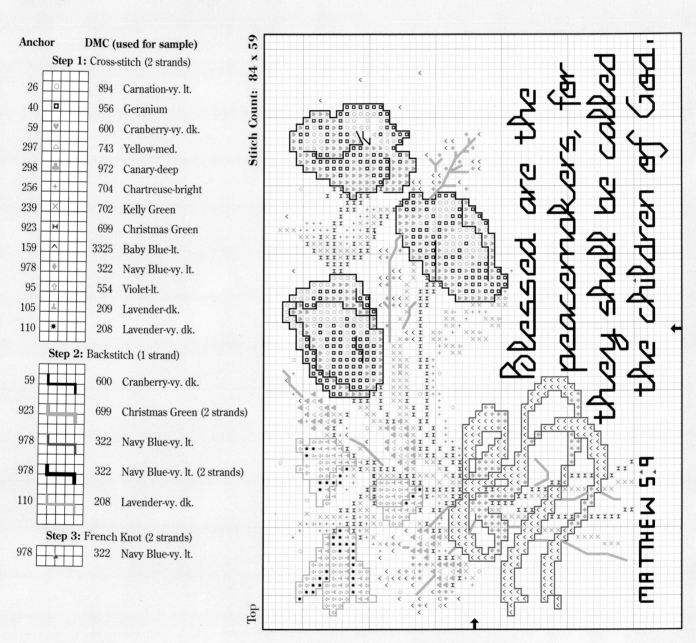

Stitch Count: 84 x 59

Top

Blessed are the peacemakers, for they shall be called the children of God.

MATTHEW 5:9

69

Plenty and Grace

Stitched on White Aida **14**, the finished design size is
5 $^{7}/_{8}$" x 8 $^{3}/_{8}$". The fabric was cut **12**" x **15**".

Fabric	Design Size
Aida **11**	7 $^{1}/_{2}$" x 10 $^{5}/_{8}$"
Aida **18**	4 $^{5}/_{8}$" x 6 $^{1}/_{2}$"
Hardanger **22**	3 $^{3}/_{4}$" x 5 $^{3}/_{8}$"

Anchor		DMC (used for sample)	

Step 1: Cross-stitch (2 strands)

Anchor		DMC	
894	+	223	Shell Pink-med.
896	♥	3721	Shell Pink-dk.
8	▫	3824	Apricot-lt.
890	✕	729	Old Gold-med.
243	◇	988	Forest Green-med.
246	✚	319	Pistachio Green-vy. dk.
160	△	813	Blue-lt.
978	⋈	322	Navy Blue-vy. lt.
363	⊥	436	Tan
8581	∧	647	Beaver Gray-med.
400	▲	414	Steel Gray-dk.
403	●	310	Black

Step 2: Backstitch (1 strand)

Anchor	DMC	
246	319	Pistachio Green-vy. dk. (2 strands)
363	436	Tan
8581	647	Beaver Gray-med. (2 strands)
403	310	Black
403	310	Black (2 strands)

Step 3: French Knot (1 strand)

Anchor	DMC	
896	3721	Shell Pink-dk.
403	310	Black (2 strands)

Alternate Verse

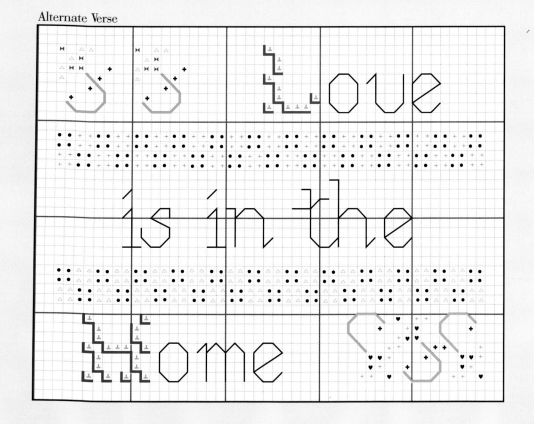

71

All creatures great
and small
The Lord God made
them all

All Creatures

Stitched on Ivory Aida 14, the finished design size is 8 ⅝" x 16 ⅛". The fabric was cut 15" x 22".

Fabrics   **Design Size**
Aida 11   11" x 20 ½"
Aida 18   6 ¾" x 12 ½"
Hardanger 22   5 ½" x 10 ¼"

Stitch Count: 83 x 117

Anchor   **DMC (used for sample)**

Step 1: Cross-stitch (2 strands)

Anchor		DMC	
48	+	818	Baby Pink
25	♡	3326	Rose-lt.
323	&	722	Orange Spice-lt.
297	⇩	743	Yellow-med.
256	%	704	Chartreuse-bright
265	=	3348	Yellow Green-lt.
257	◇	3346	Hunter Green
258	▲	904	Parrot Green-vy. dk.
158	∨	775	Baby Blue-vy. lt.
160	⋈	813	Blue-lt.
95	✕	554	Violet-lt.
387	○	712	Cream
886	▽	677	Old Gold-vy. lt.
347	✳	402	Mahogany-vy. lt.
892	⇩	3770	Peach Pecan-vy. lt.
313	✿	3825	Pale Pumpkin
338	◻	3776	Mahogany-lt.
351	♥	400	Mahogany-dk.
376	+	842	Beige Brown-vy. lt.
378	◻	841	Beige Brown-lt.
380	◆	839	Beige Brown-dk.
357	●	801	Coffee Brown-dk.
397	⊤	762	Pearl Gray-vy. lt.
398	╲	415	Pearl Gray
399	■	318	Steel Gray-lt.
403	✕	310	Black
1	○		White

Step 2: Backstitch (1 strand)

Anchor		DMC	
258		904	Parrot Green-vy. dk.
978		322	Navy Blue-vy. lt.
351		400	Mahogany-dk.
357		801	Coffee Brown-dk.
400		414	Steel Gray-dk.
403		310	Black

Step 3: Straight Stitch (1 strand)

Anchor		DMC	
258		904	Parrot Green-vy. dk.
400		414	Steel Gray-dk. —cat's whiskers
351		400	Mahogany-dk.
357		801	Coffee Brown-dk.

Step 4: French Knot (2 strands)

Anchor		DMC	
351		400	Mahogany-dk.
357	●	801	Coffee Brown-dk.
403	●	310	Black

Top

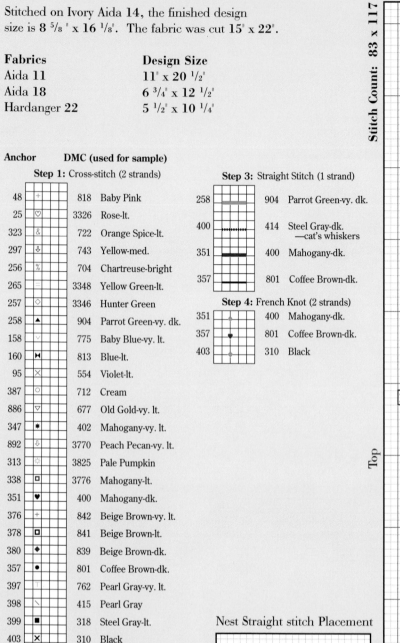

Nest Straight stitch Placement

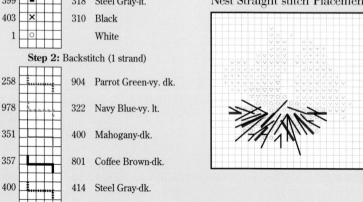

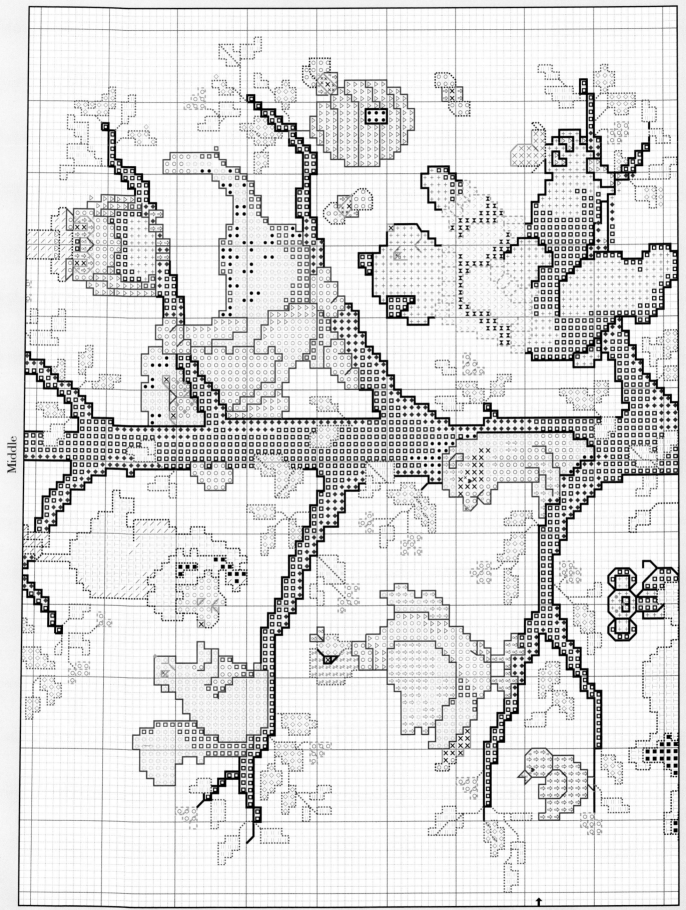

Middle

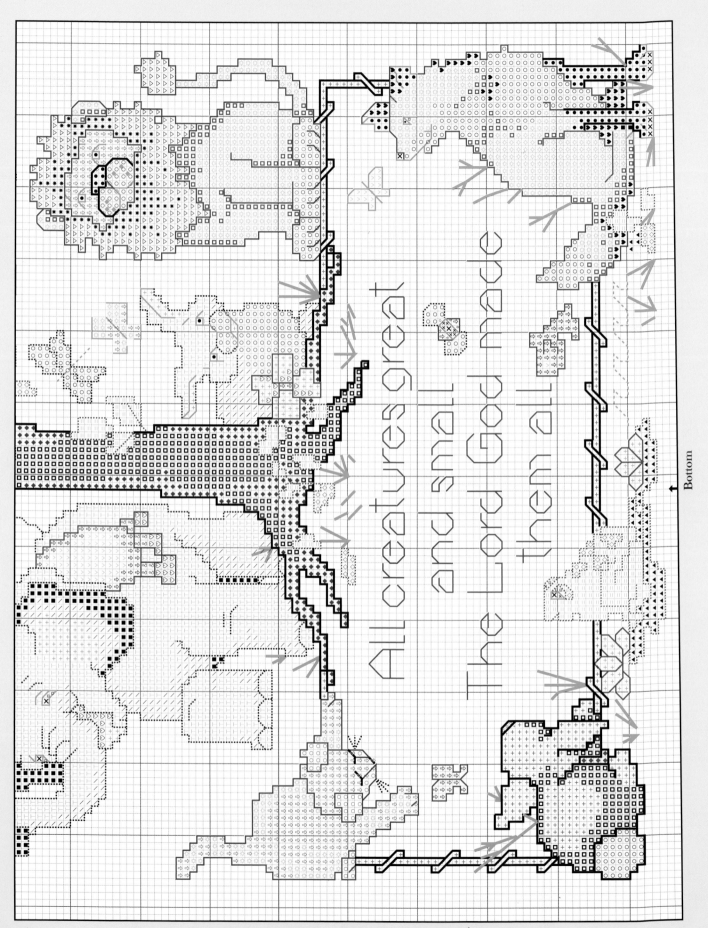

All creatures great
and small ...
The Lord God made
them all ...

Bottom

The 23rd Psalm

Stitched on White Aida 14, the finished design size is $9\,^3/_8$" x $12\,^1/_2$". The fabric was cut 16' x 19'.

Fabric	Design Size
Aida 11	12" x 15 $^7/_8$"
Aida 18	7 $^3/_8$" x 9 $^3/_4$"
Hardanger 22	6" x 8"

Anchor **DMC (used for sample)**

Step 1: Cross-stitch (2 strands)

316	♥	970	Pumpkin-lt.
306	✚	725	Topaz
206	↰	955	Nile Green-lt.
242	⌘	989	Forest Green
862	▼	935	Avocado Green-dk.
159	☆	3325	Baby Blue-lt.
130	╱	799	Delft-med.
132	✳	797	Royal Blue
110	✕	208	Lavender-vy. dk.
8581	W	647	Beaver Gray-med.
400	●	414	Steel Gray-dk.

Step 2: Backstitch (1 strand)

403		310	Black
132		797	Royal Blue

Step 3: French Knot (2 strands)

403	◆	310	Black

Top Right

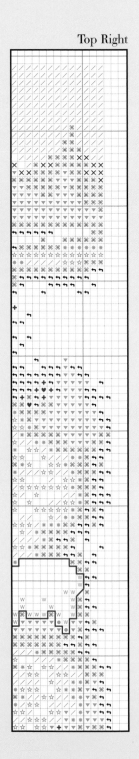

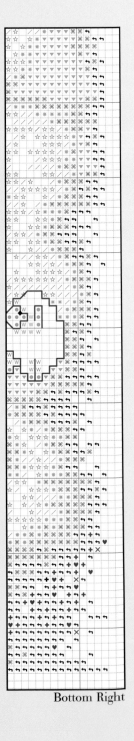

Bottom Right

78

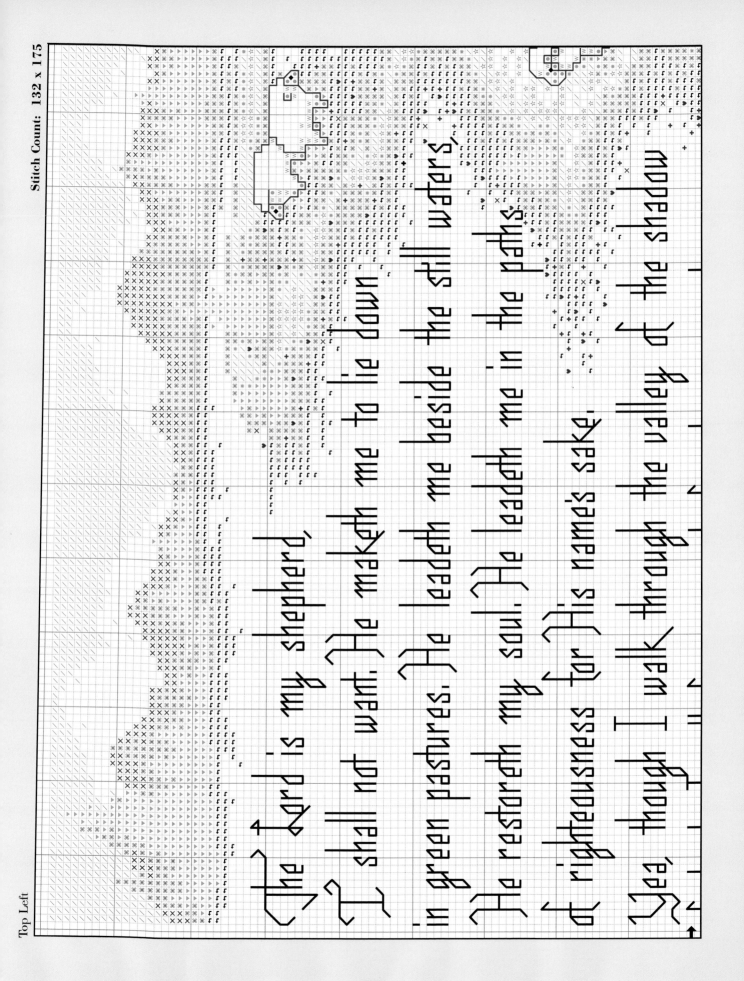

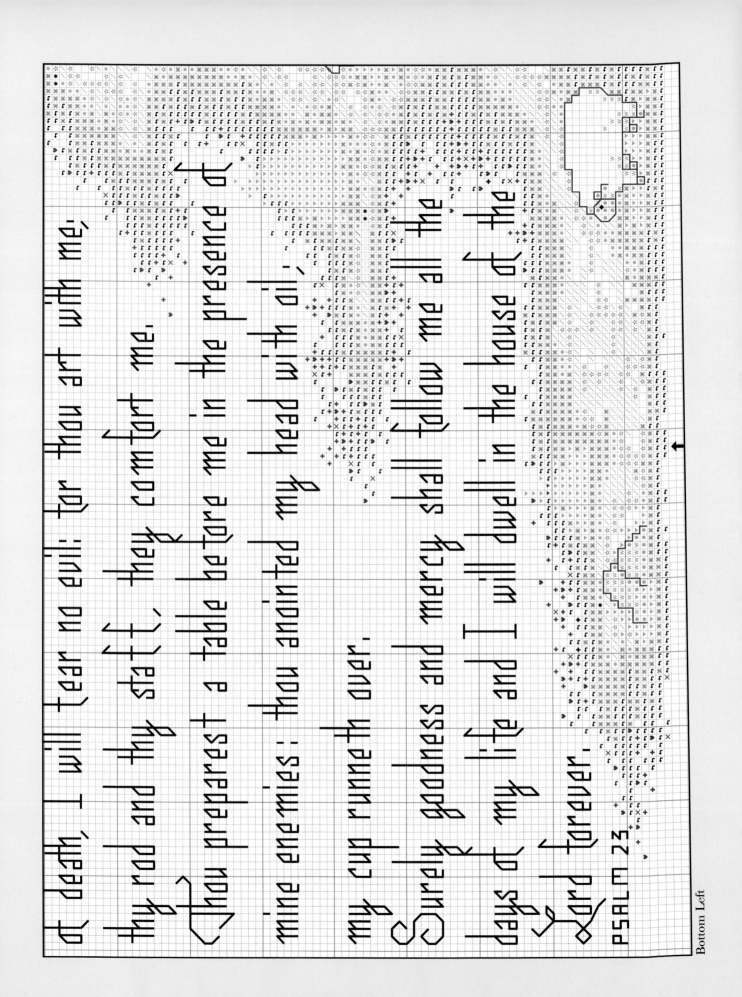

The Lord is My Shepherd Bible Cover

Stitched on Ivory Aida 14, the finished design size is 12" x 7 5/8". The fabric was cut 18" x 14".

Fabrics	**Design Size**
Aida 11	15 1/4" x 9 5/8"
Aida 18	9 3/8" x 5 7/8"
Hardanger 22	7 5/8" x 4 7/8"

Bible Cover Finishing Instructions

1. To make the pattern for the cover; measure the vertical length of your Bible along the spine. Add **1"** to this length for the seam allowance and record the measurement. Cut an **18"** length of paper to the height of the recorded measurement. Center the pattern on the Aida and a coordinating piece of backing fabric (making sure there is an equal amount of space above and below the cross-stitched border), pin and cut both out.

2. Pin the backing fabric and the Aida together with the right sides facing. Sew together with a 1/2" seam allowance leaving an opening for turning, **not near a corner**. Turn right side out. Slip-stitch the opening closed.

3. Center the cross-stitched cross on the spine of the Bible. Fold the front and back cover against the Bible. Open the front and back covers of the Bible and fold the excess material in to create a flap. Close the Bible to assure a good fit and slip-stitch the edges together around the Bible jacket.

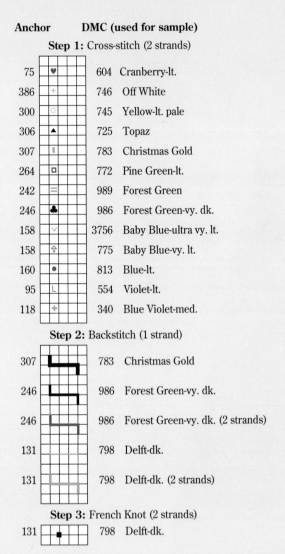

Anchor		DMC	(used for sample)
Step 1: Cross-stitch (2 strands)			
75	♥	604	Cranberry-lt.
386	+	746	Off White
300		745	Yellow-lt. pale
306	▲	725	Topaz
307		783	Christmas Gold
264	□	772	Pine Green-lt.
242	=	989	Forest Green
246	♣	986	Forest Green-vy. dk.
158	∨	3756	Baby Blue-ultra vy. lt.
158	⇧	775	Baby Blue-vy. lt.
160	●	813	Blue-lt.
95	L	554	Violet-lt.
118	✢	340	Blue Violet-med.
Step 2: Backstitch (1 strand)			
307		783	Christmas Gold
246		986	Forest Green-vy. dk.
246		986	Forest Green-vy. dk. (2 strands)
131		798	Delft-dk.
131		798	Delft-dk. (2 strands)
Step 3: French Knot (2 strands)			
131	■	798	Delft-dk.

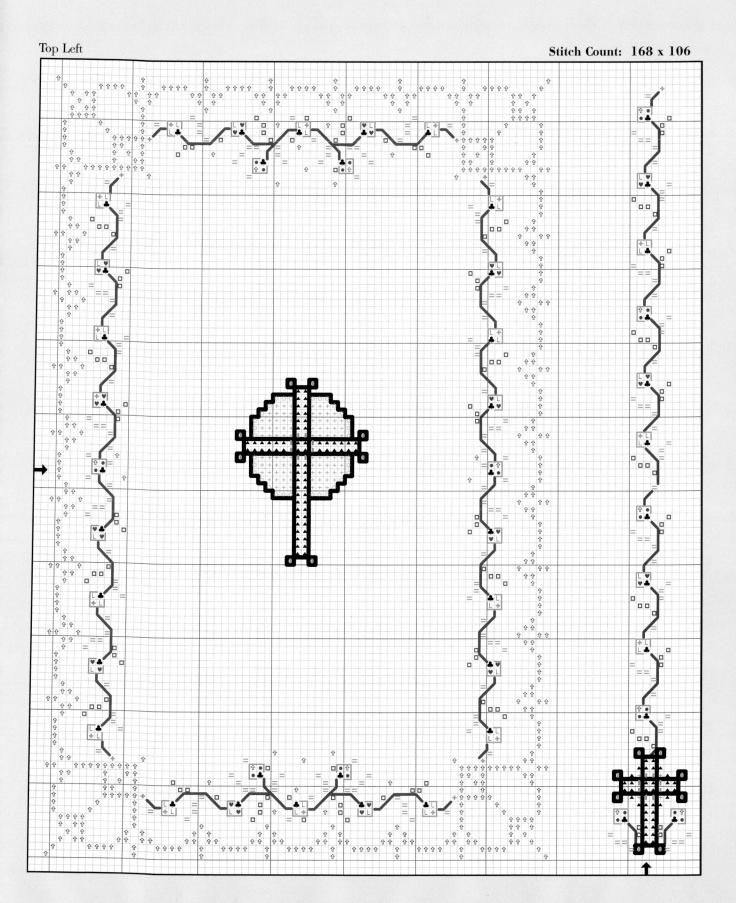

The Lord is my shepherd I shall not want ...

The Lord's Prayer

Stitched on Ivory Aida **14**, the finished design size is **8 ⁷⁄₈" x 11 ⁵⁄₈"**. The fabric was cut **15" x 18"**.

Fabrics   **Design Size**

Aida **11**   **11 ³⁄₈" x 14 ³⁄₄"**

Aida **18**   **7" x 9"**

Hardanger **22**   **5 ⁵⁄₈" x 7 ³⁄₈"**

Anchor   **DMC (used for sample)**

Step 1: Cross-stitch (2 strands)

Anchor		DMC	
300	o	745	Yellow-lt. pale
306	T	725	Topaz
890	◥	729	Old Gold-med.
243	ß	988	Forest Green-med.
258	✿	904	Parrot Green-vy. dk.
167	♡	3766	Peacock Blue-lt.
158	∴	775	Baby Blue-vy. lt.
128	◆	800	Delft-pale
154	✕	3755	Baby Blue
162	■	825	Blue-dk.

Step 2: Backstitch (1 strand)

Anchor		DMC	
246		319	Pistachio Green-vy. dk.
246		319	Pistachio Green-vy. dk. (2 strands)
162		825	Blue-dk.
162		825	Blue-dk. (2 strands)—words

Step 3: French Knot (2 strands)

Anchor		DMC	
162	●	825	Blue-dk.

Optional Alphabet for Capital Letters

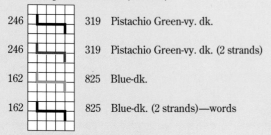

Top

Our Father who art in heaven, hallowed be Thy name. Thy kingdom come. Thy will be done, on earth as it is in heaven. Give us this day our daily bread, and forgive us our trespasses, as we forgive those who trespass against us.

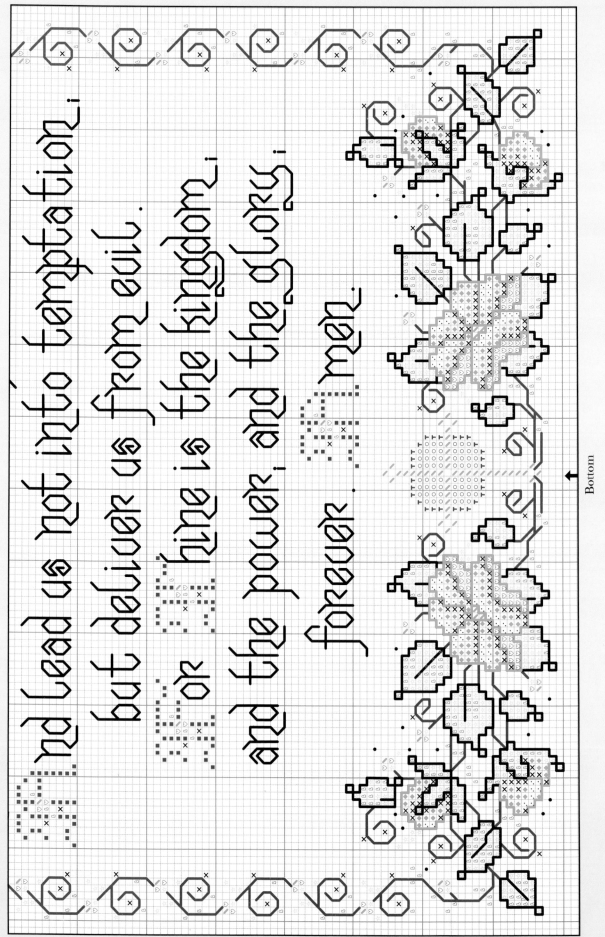

nd lead us not into temptation,
but deliver us from evil.
For Thine is the kingdom,
and the power, and the glory,
forever. Amen.

Bottom

88

God Bless Our Home

Stitched on Cream Aida **14**, the finished design size is 6 ⅝" x 4 ⅝". The fabric was cut **13"** x **11"**. See Ribbon Embroidery Instructions on page **127**.

Fabrics

Fabrics	Design Size
Aida 11	8 ½" x 5 ⅞"
Aida 18	5 ⅛" x 3 ⅝"
Hardanger 22	4 ¼" x 3"

Supplies Required for Silk Ribbon Embroidery
Silk embroidery ribbon:
- 2 yds. of Peach 4mm
- 2 yds. of Coral 4mm
- 2 yds. of Burgundy 4mm
- 1 yd. of Pale Yellow 4mm
- 2 yds. of Lime Green 4mm
- 2 yds. of Green 4mm
- 3 yds. of Blue 4mm

DMC floss:
- 3325 Baby Blue-lt.

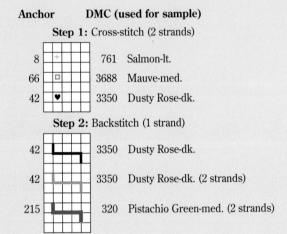

Anchor		DMC (used for sample)	
Step 1: Cross-stitch (2 strands)			
8	+	761	Salmon-lt.
66	□	3688	Mauve-med.
42	♥	3350	Dusty Rose-dk.
Step 2: Backstitch (1 strand)			
42		3350	Dusty Rose-dk.
42		3350	Dusty Rose-dk. (2 strands)
215		320	Pistachio Green-med. (2 strands)

Top

Stitch Count: 93 x 65

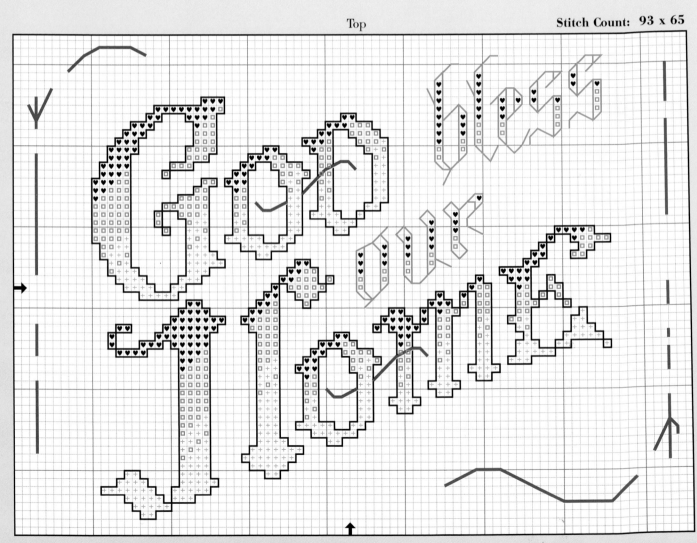

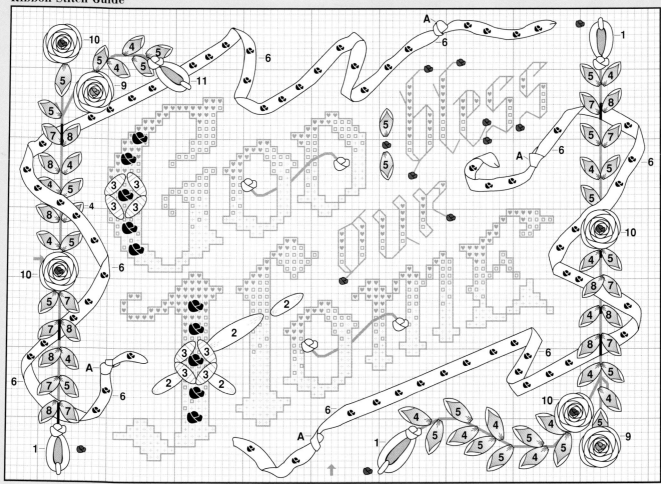

Ribbon Embroidery Guide

Buds **1** - Burgundy Decorative Lazy Daisy with Coral center.
Letter "H" **2** - Burgundy Straight Stitch.
Buds **3** - Pale Yellow Straight Whip Stitch.
Leaves **4** - Lime Green Japanese Ribbon Stitch.
Leaves **5** - Green Japanese Ribbon Stitch.
Ribbon **6** - Blue Tacked Ribbon Stitch (knot the ribbon at A) couched with Baby Blue-lt. DMC floss (2 strands)
     French Knots.
Leaves **7** - Lime Green Japanese Ribbon Stitch.
Leaves **8** - Green Japanese Ribbon Stitch.
Flowers **9** - Burgundy Decorative Spider Web Rose with Coral outer petals and Peach French Knot center.
Flowers **10** - Coral Decorative Spider Web Rose with Peach outer petals and Burgundy French Knot center.
Bud **11**- Coral Decorative Lazy Daisy with Burgundy Straight Stitch center.

Detail
Buds - Burgundy French Knots (small dark grey knots).
Buds - Green French Knots (large white knots).
Buds - Blue French Knots (large black knots).
Stems - Finish stems with Pistachio Green-med. DMC floss (2 strands) Backstitch (bold black lines).

Celestial Angel

Stitched on Cream Murano **30** over **2** threads, the finished design size is **9 3/8" x 11 5/8"**. The fabric was cut **16" x 18"**.

Fabrics	Design Size
Aida **11**	12 7/8" x 15 7/8"
Aida **14**	10 1/8" x 12 1/2"
Aida **18**	7 7/8" x 9 3/4"
Hardanger **22**	6 3/8" x 8"

Anchor   **DMC (used for sample)**

Step 1: Cross-stitch (2 strands)

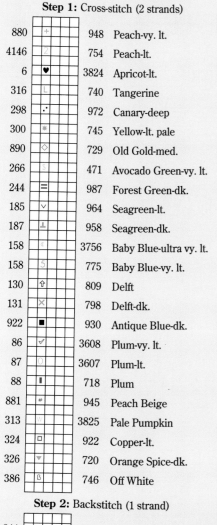

880	948	Peach-vy. lt.
4146	754	Peach-lt.
6	3824	Apricot-lt.
316	740	Tangerine
298	972	Canary-deep
300	745	Yellow-lt. pale
890	729	Old Gold-med.
266	471	Avocado Green-vy. lt.
244	987	Forest Green-dk.
185	964	Seagreen-lt.
187	958	Seagreen-dk.
158	3756	Baby Blue-ultra vy. lt.
158	775	Baby Blue-vy. lt.
130	809	Delft
131	798	Delft-dk.
922	930	Antique Blue-dk.
86	3608	Plum-vy. lt.
87	3607	Plum-lt.
88	718	Plum
881	945	Peach Beige
313	3825	Pale Pumpkin
324	922	Copper-lt.
326	720	Orange Spice-dk.
386	746	Off White

Step 2: Backstitch (1 strand)

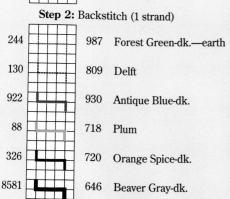

244	987	Forest Green-dk.—earth
130	809	Delft
922	930	Antique Blue-dk.
88	718	Plum
326	720	Orange Spice-dk.
8581	646	Beaver Gray-dk.

Optional Alphabet for Personalization

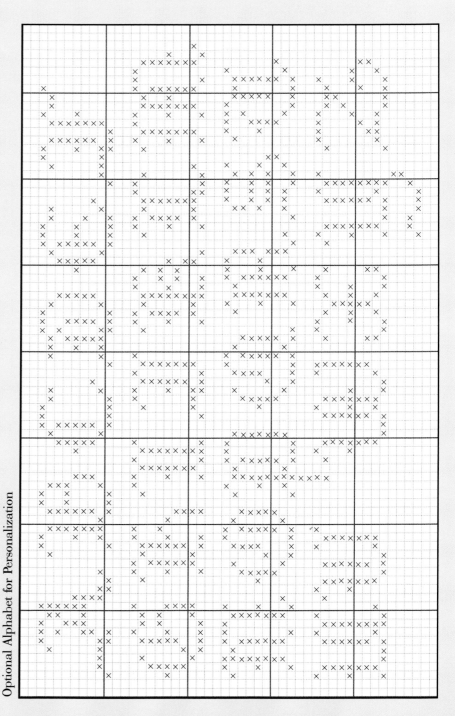

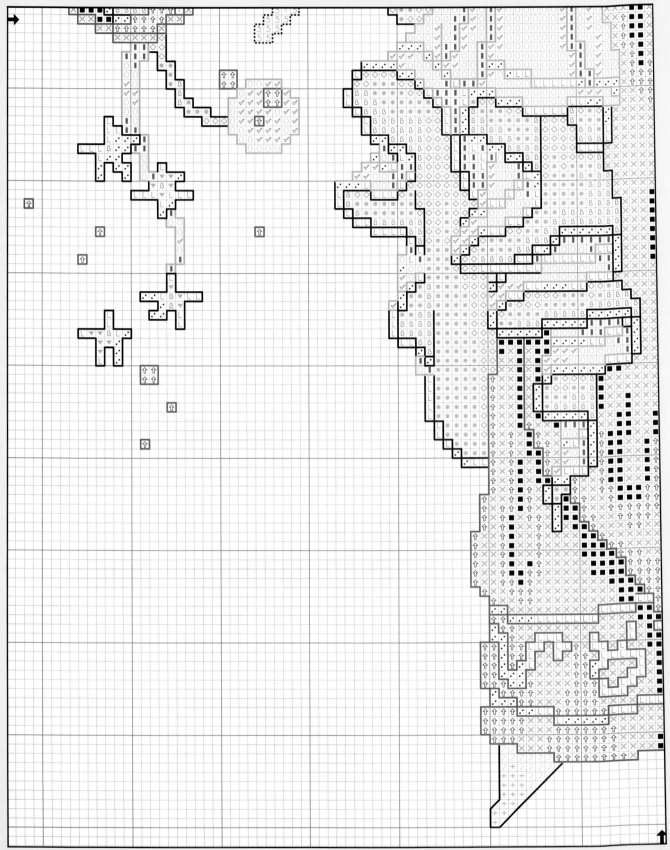

Bottom Left

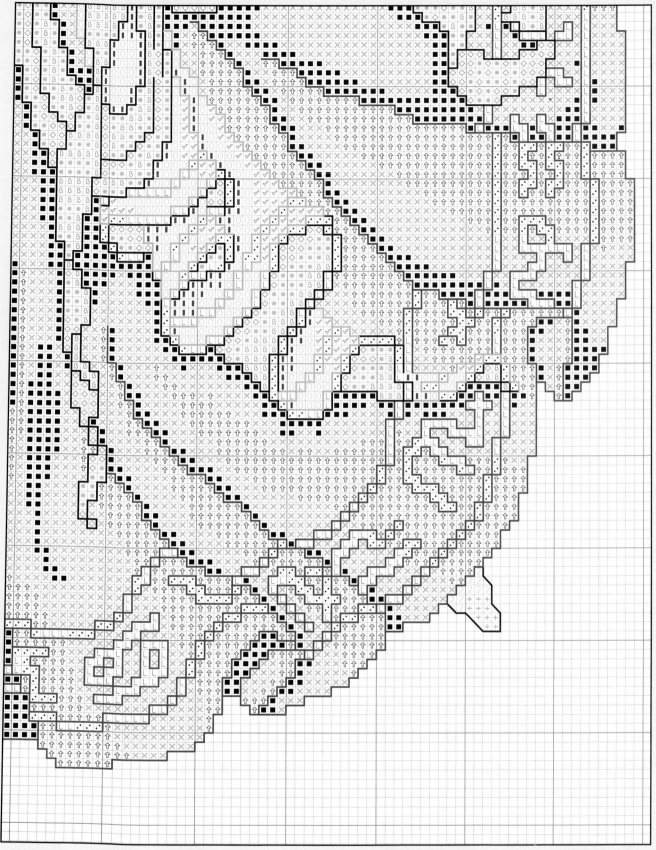

Bottom Right

PATIENCE

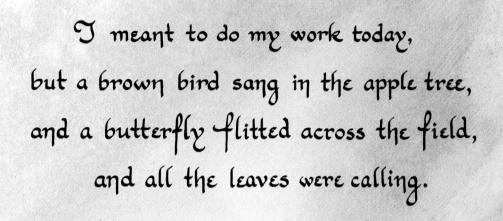

I meant to do my work today,
but a brown bird sang in the apple tree,
and a butterfly flitted across the field,
and all the leaves were calling.

RICHARD LA GALLIENN

Serenity Prayer

Stitched on White Aida 14, the finished design
size is 9 ³/₈" x 12 ¹/₄". The fabric was cut 16" x 19".

Fabrics	Design size
Aida 11	12" x 15 ¹/₂"
Aida 18	7 ³/₈" x 9 ¹/₂"
Hardanger 22	6" x 7 ³/₄"

Anchor   **DMC (used for sample)**

Step 1: Cross-stitch (2 strands)

Anchor		DMC	
316	≡	740	Tangerine
295		726	Topaz-lt.
307	✦	783	Christmas Gold
239	╱	702	Kelly Green
923	♡	699	Christmas Green
879	⋈	890	Pistachio Green-ultra dk.
159		3325	Baby Blue-lt.
131	×	798	Delft-dk.
118	◇	340	Blue Violet-med.
338	⊥	3776	Mahogany-lt.
371	○	433	Brown-med.
382	■	3371	Black Brown
403	✳	310	Black

Step 2: Backstitch (1 strand)

Anchor	DMC	
879	890	Pistachio Green-ultra dk.
879	890	Pistachio Green-ultra dk. (2 strands)
371	433	Brown-med. (2 strands)
382	3371	Black Brown
382	3371	Black Brown (2 strands)
403	310	Black

Step 3: Straight Stitch (2 strands)

Anchor	DMC	
879	890	Pistachio Green-ultra dk.
403	310	Black

Step 4: French Knot (2 strands)

Anchor	DMC	
382	3371	Black Brown
403	310	Black

Top Right Side

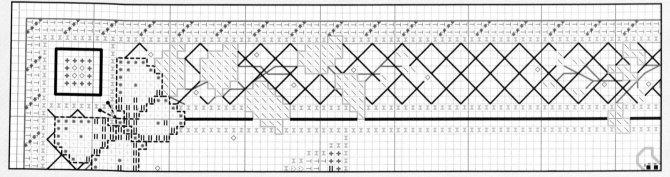

Bottom Right Side

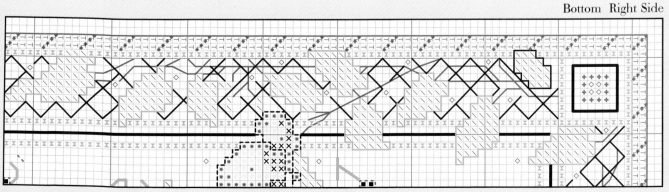

Top Left Side

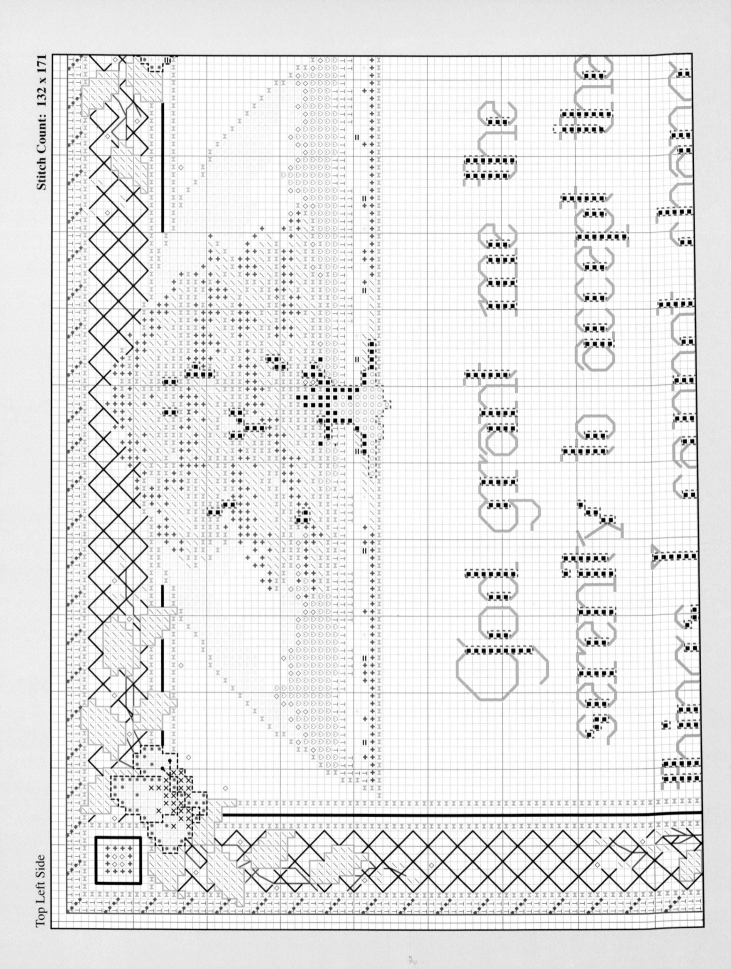

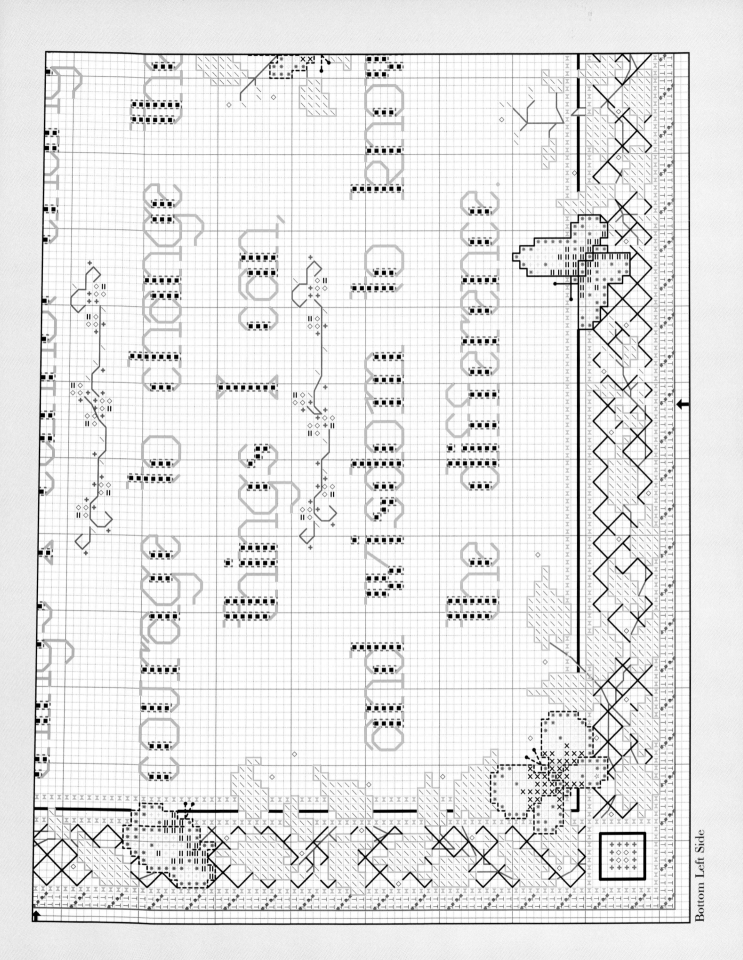

Our Father Bible Cover

Stitched on Cream Aida 14, the finished design size is 11 ³/₈" x 7 ⁵/₈". The fabric was cut 18" x 14".

Fabrics	Design Size
Aida 11	14 ¹/₂" x 9 ⁵/₈"
Aida 18	8 ⁷/₈" x 5 ⁷/₈"
Hardanger 22	7 ¹/₄" x 4 ⁷/₈"

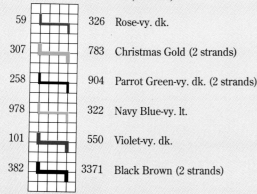

Anchor		DMC (used for sample)	
Step 1: Cross-stitch (2 strands)			
25	∨	3326	Rose-lt.
42	$	335	Rose
59	⊥	326	Rose-vy. dk.
307	+	783	Christmas Gold
265	○	3348	Yellow Green-lt.
266	★	3347	Yellow Green-med.
258	◆	904	Parrot Green-vy. dk.
159	∴	3325	Baby Blue-lt.
105	#	209	Lavender-dk.
382	■	3371	Black Brown
Step 2: Backstitch (1 strand)			
59		326	Rose-vy. dk.
307		783	Christmas Gold (2 strands)
258		904	Parrot Green-vy. dk. (2 strands)
978		322	Navy Blue-vy. lt.
101		550	Violet-vy. dk.
382		3371	Black Brown (2 strands)
Step 3: French Knot (2 strands)			
382	♥	3371	Black Brown

Bible Cover Finishing Instructions

1. To make the pattern for the cover; measure the vertical length of your Bible along the spine. Add 1" to this length for the seam allowance and record the measurement. Cut an 18" length of paper to the height of the recorded measurement. Center the pattern on the Aida and a coordinating piece of backing fabric (making sure there is an equal amount of space above and below the cross-stitched border), pin and cut both out.

2. Pin the backing fabric and Aida together with right sides facing. Sew together with a ¹/₂" seam allowance leaving an opening for turning, **not near a corner.** Turn right side out. Slip-stitch the opening closed.

3. Center the cross-stitched cross on the spine of the Bible. Fold the front and back cover against the Bible. Open the front and back covers of the Bible and fold the excess material in to create a flap. Close the Bible to assure a good fit and slip-stitch the edges together around the Bible jacket.

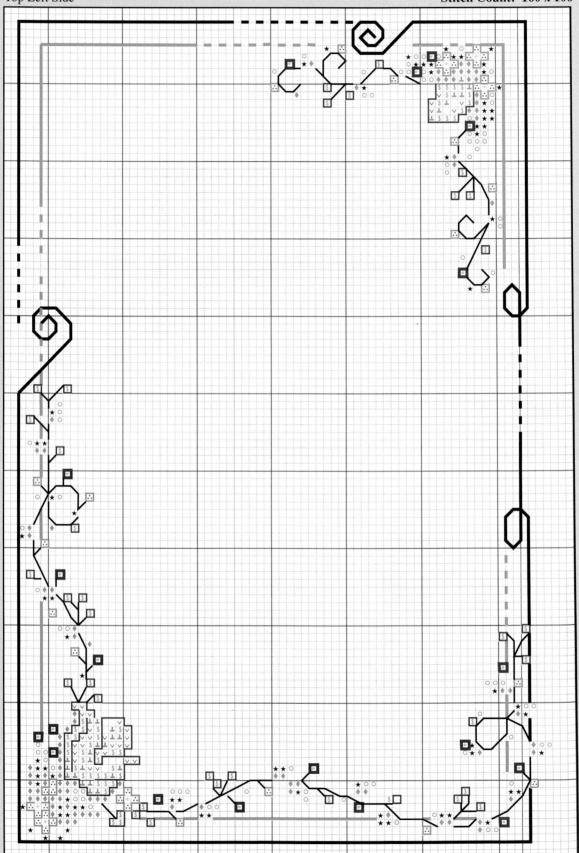

Our Father who art in heaven hallowed be thy name

Our Father Sampler

Stitched on Vintage Linen 28 over 2 threads, the finished design size is 9 ¼" x 12 ⅛". The fabric was cut 16" x 19".

Fabrics   **Design Size**
Aida 11   11 ⅞" x 15 ½"
Aida 18   7 ¼" x 9 ½"
Hardanger 22   5 ⅞" x 7 ¾"

Anchor   **DMC (used for sample)**

Step 1: Cross-stitch (2 strands)

Anchor		DMC	
25	╱	3326	Rose-lt.
42		335	Rose
59	♥	326	Rose-vy. dk.
307	✕	783	Christmas Gold
265	✳	3348	Yellow Green-lt.
243	△	988	Forest Green-med.
258	⋈	904	Parrot Green-vy. dk.
159	○	3325	Baby Blue-lt.
105	+	209	Lavender-dk.
382	■	3371	Black Brown

Step 2: Backstitch (1 strand)

Anchor		DMC	
59		326	Rose-vy. dk.
307		783	Christmas Gold (2 strands)
258		904	Parrot Green-vy. dk.
978		322	Navy Blue-vy. lt.
101		550	Violet-vy. dk.
382		3371	Black Brown (2 strands)

Step 3: French Knot (2 strands)

Anchor		DMC	
382		3371	Black Brown

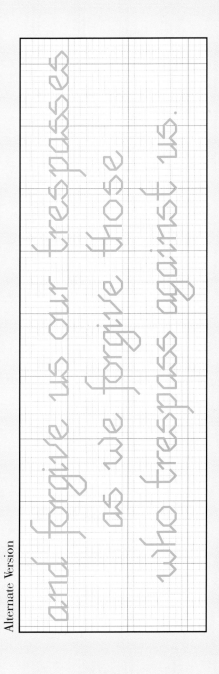

Alternate Version

109

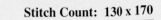

as we

our de

And lead us not

but deliver

For time is t

the pou

the glory fore

MATTHEW 6-9-13

All Things Are Possible

Stitched on White Aida **14**, the finished design size is **4"** x **6 ⅛"**. The fabric was cut **10"** x **12"**.

Fabrics	Design size
Aida **11**	5 ⅛" x 7 ¾"
Aida **18**	3 ⅛" x 4 ¾"
Hardanger **22**	2 ½" x 3 ⅞"

Stitch Count: 56 x 85

Anchor   DMC (used for sample)

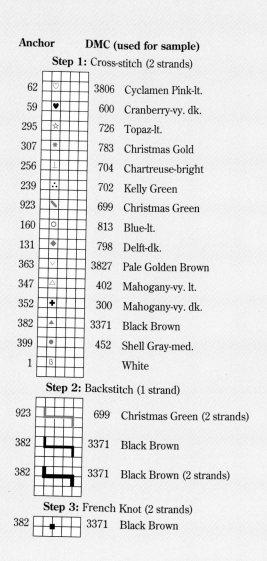

Step 1: Cross-stitch (2 strands)

Anchor		DMC	
62	♡	3806	Cyclamen Pink-lt.
59	♥	600	Cranberry-vy. dk.
295	☆	726	Topaz-lt.
307	✳	783	Christmas Gold
256	⊥	704	Chartreuse-bright
239	∴	702	Kelly Green
923	◥	699	Christmas Green
160	○	813	Blue-lt.
131	◆	798	Delft-dk.
363	⋎	3827	Pale Golden Brown
347	△	402	Mahogany-vy. lt.
352	✚	300	Mahogany-vy. dk.
382	▲	3371	Black Brown
399	●	452	Shell Gray-med.
1	ß		White

Step 2: Backstitch (1 strand)

923		699	Christmas Green (2 strands)
382		3371	Black Brown
382		3371	Black Brown (2 strands)

Step 3: French Knot (2 strands)

382	■	3371	Black Brown

The Lord is My Shepherd

Stitched on White Aida 14, the finished design size is 4 1/8" x 6 1/8". The fabric was cut 10" x 12".

Fabrics	Design size
Aida 11	5 1/8" x 7 7/8"
Aida 18	3 1/8" x 4 3/4"
Hardanger 22	2 5/8" x 3 7/8"

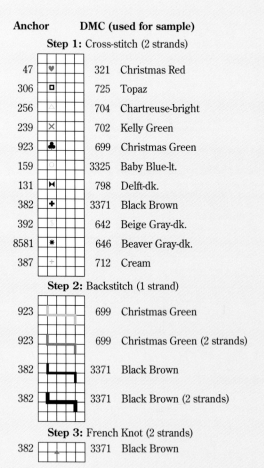

Anchor		DMC (used for sample)	
Step 1: Cross-stitch (2 strands)			
47	♥	321	Christmas Red
306	▫	725	Topaz
256		704	Chartreuse-bright
239	×	702	Kelly Green
923	♣	699	Christmas Green
159		3325	Baby Blue-lt.
131	⋈	798	Delft-dk.
382	✦	3371	Black Brown
392		642	Beige Gray-dk.
8581	✳	646	Beaver Gray-dk.
387	+	712	Cream
Step 2: Backstitch (1 strand)			
923		699	Christmas Green
923		699	Christmas Green (2 strands)
382		3371	Black Brown
382		3371	Black Brown (2 strands)
Step 3: French Knot (2 strands)			
382		3371	Black Brown

Stitch Count: 57 x 86

116

In All Things

Stitched on Rustico 14, the finished design size
is 8 ¹/₈" x 11 ¹/₈". The fabric was cut 15" x 18".

Fabrics	Design size
Aida 11	10 ¹/₄" x 14 ¹/₈"
Aida 18	6 ¹/₄" x 8 ⁵/₈"
Hardanger 22	5 ¹/₈" x 7 ¹/₈"

Anchor **DMC (used for sample)**

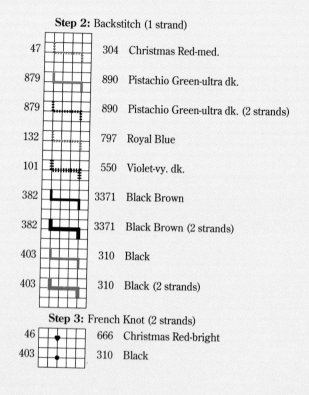

Step 1: Cross-stitch (2 strands)

Anchor		DMC	
48		818	Baby Pink
27		899	Rose-med.
46		666	Christmas Red-bright
47		304	Christmas Red-med.
295		726	Topaz-lt.
298		972	Canary-deep
208		563	Jade-lt.
210		562	Jade-med.
879		890	Pistachio Green-ultra dk.
159		3325	Baby Blue-lt.
130		799	Delft-med.
132		797	Royal Blue
108		211	Lavender-lt.
98		553	Violet-med.
101		550	Violet-vy. dk.
376		842	Beige Brown-vy. lt.
378		841	Beige Brown-lt.
380		839	Beige Brown-dk.
398		415	Pearl Gray
399		318	Steel Gray-lt.
403		310	Black

Step 2: Backstitch (1 strand)

Anchor		DMC	
47		304	Christmas Red-med.
879		890	Pistachio Green-ultra dk.
879		890	Pistachio Green-ultra dk. (2 strands)
132		797	Royal Blue
101		550	Violet-vy. dk.
382		3371	Black Brown
382		3371	Black Brown (2 strands)
403		310	Black
403		310	Black (2 strands)

Step 3: French Knot (2 strands)

Anchor		DMC	
46		666	Christmas Red-bright
403		310	Black

Top

In all things
of Nature
there is something

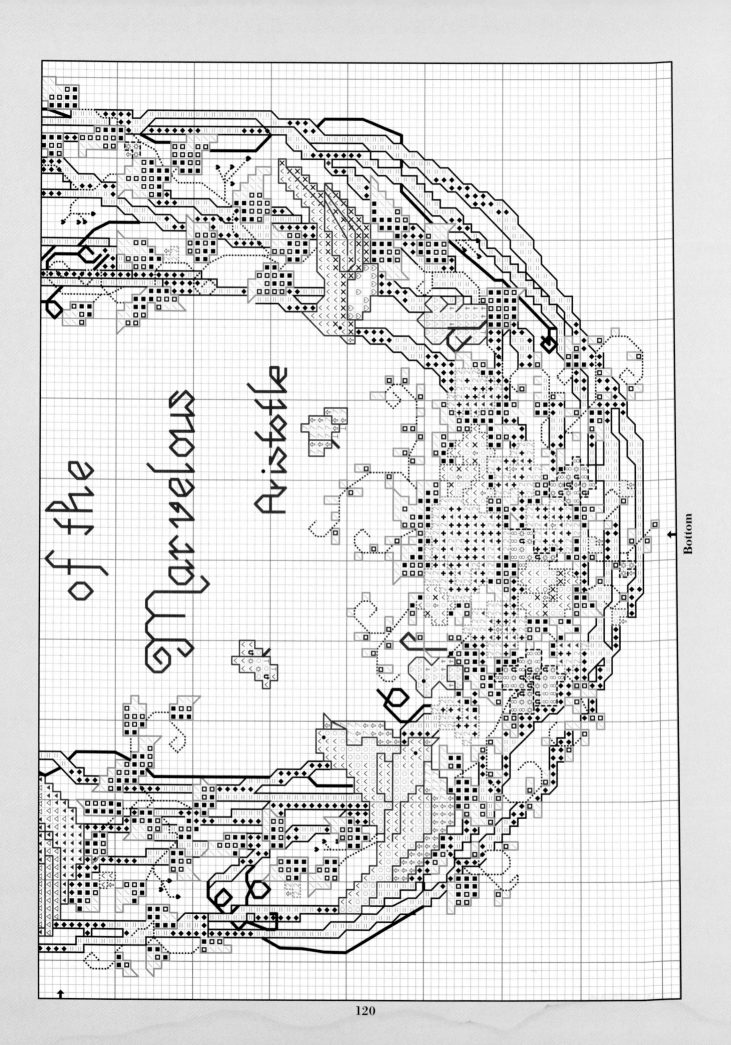

Bottom

Love is patient, love is kind.
Love is not jealous or boastful;
it is not arrogant or rude.
Love does not insist on its own way
it is not irritable or resentful;
it does not rejoice at wrong
but rejoices in the right.
Love bears all things, believes
all things, hopes all things,
endures all things. Love never ends.
ST. PAUL TO THE CORINTHIANS

St. Paul to the Corinthians

Stitched on Cream Aida 14, the finished design size is 10 ⅝" x 13 ⅜". The fabric was cut 17" x 20".

Fabrics	Design Size
Aida 11	13 ½" x 17 ⅛"
Aida 18	8 ¼" x 10 ½"
Hardanger 22	6 ¾" x 8 ½"

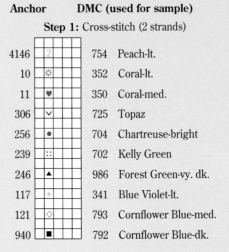

Anchor		DMC (used for sample)	
Step 1: Cross-stitch (2 strands)			
4146	2	754	Peach-lt.
10	☼	352	Coral-lt.
11	♥	350	Coral-med.
306	∨	725	Topaz
256	●	704	Chartreuse-bright
239	∷	702	Kelly Green
246	▲	986	Forest Green-vy. dk.
117	+	341	Blue Violet-lt.
121	◇	793	Cornflower Blue-med.
940	■	792	Cornflower Blue-dk.

Top Left

Stitch Count: 149 x 188

122

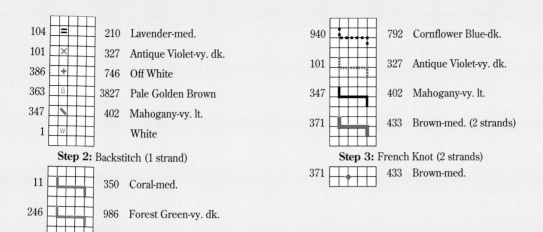

104	=	210	Lavender-med.
101	×	327	Antique Violet-vy. dk.
386	+	746	Off White
363	ß	3827	Pale Golden Brown
347	◣	402	Mahogany-vy. lt.
1	W		White

Step 2: Backstitch (1 strand)

11		350	Coral-med.
246		986	Forest Green-vy. dk.

940		792	Cornflower Blue-dk.
101		327	Antique Violet-vy. dk.
347		402	Mahogany-vy. lt.
371		433	Brown-med. (2 strands)

Step 3: French Knot (2 strands)

371	◆	433	Brown-med.

Top Right

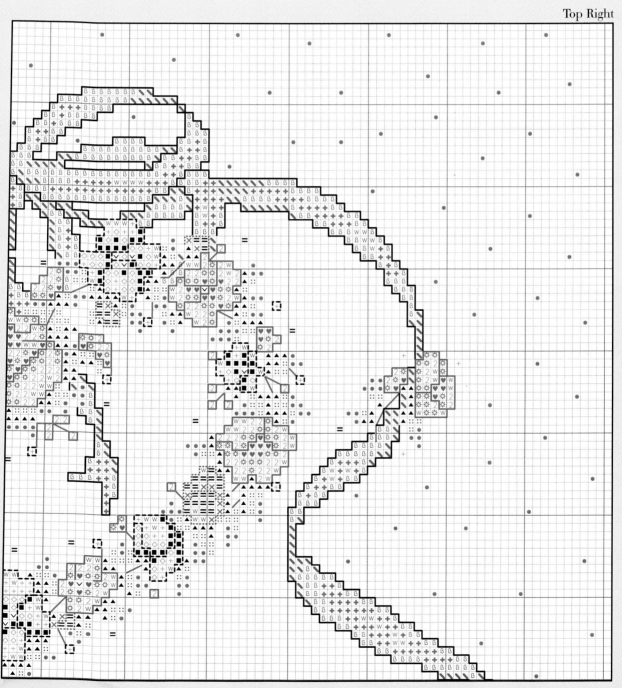

123

ent, love is kind.

alous, or boastful;

ogant or rude

sist on its own way

e or resentful;

oice at wrong

n the right.

things, believes

s all things,

Love never ends.

ST. PAUL TO THE CORINTHIANS

Bottom Right

Cross-stitch General Instructions

Fabrics

Counted cross-stitch is usually worked on even-weave fabrics. These fabrics are manufactured specifically for counted-thread embroidery and are woven with the same number of vertical as horizontal threads per inch. Because the number of threads in the fabric is equal in each direction, each stitch will be the same size. It is the number of threads per inch in even-weave fabrics that determines the size of a finished design. Fabrics used for models are identified in sample informations by color, name, and thread count per inch.

Preparing fabric

Cut fabric at least 3" larger on all sides than finished design size or cut as indicated in sample information to ensure enough space for project assembly. A 3" margin is the minimum amount of space that allows for comfortably working the edges of the design. To prevent fraying, whipstitch or machine zigzag along raw edges or apply liquid ravel preventer.

Needles

Needles should slip easily through fabric holes without piercing fabric threads. For fabric with 11 or fewer threads per inch, use needle size 24; for 14 threads per inch, use needle size 24 or 26; for 18 or more threads per inch, use needle size 26. Never leave needle in design area of fabric. It may leave rust or permanent impression on fabric.

Floss

All numbers and color names are cross-referenced between Anchor and DMC brands of floss. Use 18" lengths of floss. For best coverage, separate strands. Dampen with wet sponge. Then put back together number of strands called for in color code.

Centering the Design

Fold the *fabric* in half horizontally, then vertically. Place a pin in the fold point to mark the center. Locate the center of the design on the *graph* by following the vertical and horizontal arrows at the left and bottom of each graph. Begin stitching all designs at the center point of the graph and the fabric unless the instructions indicate otherwise.

Securing the Floss

Insert needle up from the underside of the fabric at starting point. Hold 1" of thread behind the fabric and stitch over it, securing with the first few stitches. To finish thread, run under four or more stitches on the back of the design. Never knot floss unless working on clothing. Another method of securing floss is the waste knot. Knot floss and insert needle from the right side of the fabric about 1" from design area. Work several stitches over the thread to secure. Cut off the knot later.

Carrying Floss

To carry floss, weave floss under the previously worked stitches on the back. Do not carry thread across any fabric that is not or will not be stitched. Loose threads, especially dark ones, will show through the fabric.

Cleaning Completed Work

When stitching is complete, soak it in cold water with a mild soap for five to ten minutes. Rinse well and roll in a towel to remove excess water. Do not wring. Place work face down on a dry towel and iron on warm setting until dry.

Cross-stitch

Make one cross-stitch for each symbol on chart. Bring needle up at A, down at B, up at C, down at D; see diagram. For rows, stitch across fabric from left to right to make half-crosses and then back to complete stitches.

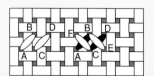

Backstitch

Complete all cross-stitching before working backstitches or other accent stitches. Working from left to right with one strand of floss (unless indicated otherwise on code), bring needle up at A, down at B, and up again at C. Go back down at A, and continue in this manner.

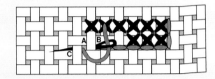

French Knot

Bring needle up at A, using one strand of embroidery floss. Wrap floss around needle two times (unless indicated otherwise in instructions). Insert needle beside A, pulling floss until it fits snugly around needle. Pull needle through to back.

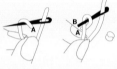

Straight Stitch

Bring needle up at A; go down at B. Pull flat. Repeat A-B for each stitch. The length of the stitch should be the same as the length of the line on the design chart.

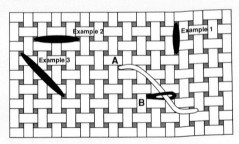

Ribbon Embroidery Instructions

Silk Ribbon

The ribbon sizes and colors are outlined in the corresponding embroidery guide. Before you begin, you should press the silk ribbon using low heat to remove any creases. Cut the ribbon into 18" lengths to reduce the chance of the silk ribbon fraying while stitching. Because of the delicate nature of silk ribbon, it can easily become worn, losing some of its body. If this happens, moisten the silk ribbon and it will self-restore.

Needles for Ribbon

The barrel of the needle must create a hole large enough for the silk ribbon to pass through. The eye of the needle must be large enough for the silk ribbon to lay flat when threaded. Use a needle pack that includes chenille needles in sizes **18** to **22**. Use a regular embroidery needle when stitching with DMC floss.

Threading and Locking Silk Ribbon

Pull about 3″ of silk ribbon through the eye of the needle. Pierce the 3″ portion of silk ribbon about ¹/₂″ from the end. Pull back on the opposite end until it locks securely around the eye of the needle; see Diagram **1**.

Diagram 1

Knotting the End of the Silk Ribbon

To create a soft knot prior to stitching, pierce the end of the silk ribbon with the needle, sliding the needle through the silk ribbon as if to make a short basting stitch. Pull the needle and silk ribbon through the stitched portion to form a knot at the ribbon end; see Diagram **2**.

Diagram 2

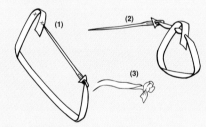

Manipulating the Silk Ribbon

One of the most important aspects of silk ribbon embroidery is manipulation of the silk ribbon. For most stitches, the silk ribbon must be kept flat, smooth and loose; see Diagram **3**. Follow the numerical order of stitches according to the stitching guide for each project.

Diagram 3

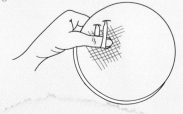

To End Stitching

Secure your stitches in place for each flower or small area before beginning a new area. Do not drag the ribbon from one area to another. Tie a slip knot on the wrong side of your needlework to secure the stitch in place and end ribbon.

Caring for Your Projects

It is recommended to spot clean only. However, you may hand-wash the design with mild dishwashing detergent. If needed, carefully press around embroidered design.

Ribbon Stitches

Decorative Lazy Daisy

(1) Bring the needle up at A. Keep the ribbon flat, untwisted and full. Put the needle down through fabric at B and up through at C, keeping the ribbon under the needle to form a loop. Pull the ribbon through, leaving the loop loose and full. To hold the loop in place, go down on other side of ribbon near C, forming a straight stitch over loop.
(2) Completed Lazy Daisy.
(3) With another ribbon color, come up at D and go down just inside the top of loop, forming a straight stitch inside lazy daisy stitch.
(4) Completed Decorative Lazy Daisy.

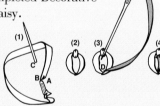

Decorative Spider Web Rose

(1) To make the french knot center; refer to French Knot on page **126**.
(2) The center can consist of a single french knot or a cluster of french knots. Using two strands of floss, securely work straight stitches to form five spokes around the outer edge of the french knot center. These are your anchor stitches to create the petals with ribbon.
(3) Bring ribbon up near the outer edge of the rose center next to one spoke. Weave the ribbon over one spoke and under the next spoke, continuing around in one direction (clockwise or counter clockwise), until

the spokes are covered. When weaving, keep the ribbon loose and allow it to twist. To end, stitch down through the fabric along the last row of petals.
(4) Completed Decorative Spider Web Rose.

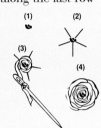

French Knot

Using ribbon, refer to French Knot on page **126**.

Japanese Ribbon Stitch

(1) Come up through fabric at the starting point of stitch. Lay the ribbon flat on the fabric. At the end of the stitch, pierce the ribbon with the needle. Slowly pull the length of the ribbon through to the back, allowing the ends of the ribbon to curl. If the ribbon is pulled too tight, the effect of the stitch can be lost. Vary the petals and leaves by adjusting the length, the tension of the ribbon before piercing and how loosely or tightly the ribbon is pulled down through itself.
(2) Completed Japanese Ribbon Stitch.

Straight Stitch

(1) Come up at A and go down at B.
(2) Completed Straight Stitch.

Straight Whip Stitch

(1) Make a straight stitch coming up at A and down at B.
(2) Come back up at A; wrap the ribbon around the straight stitch, bringing it over the top of the stitch and sliding the needle under the straight stitch. (Be careful not to catch the fabric or stitch when wrapping.) Repeat two times.
(3) Go down at C, along side of whip stitch.
(4) Completed Straight Whip Stitch.

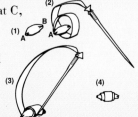

Tacked Ribbon Stitch
Use one needle threaded with ribbon (length enough to cover desired area) and another with one strand of matching color embroidery floss.
(1) With ribbon, come up from wrong side of fabric. Lay the ribbon flat in desired direction on fabric. With floss, come up through the silk ribbon and make a small straight stitch across ribbon to secure in place.
(2) To turn the ribbon flow in another direction, tack across ribbon with the floss at the point where direction is to change. The stitch should be done parallel to the fold. Fold the ribbon over the straight stitch. Continue positioning ribbon, making floss straight stitches at desired intervals. To end, stitch back down through fabric with ribbon at desired ending spot.
(3) Completed Tacked Ribbon Stitch.

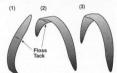

Metric Equivalence Chart

MM-Millimetres   CM-Centimetres

INCHES TO MILLIMETRES AND CENTIMETRES

INCHES	MM	CM	INCHES	CM	INCHES	CM
1/8	3	0.9	9	22.9	30	76.2
1/4	6	0.6	10	25.4	31	78.7
3/8	10	1.0	11	27.9	32	81.3
1/2	13	1.3	12	30.5	33	83.8
5/8	16	1.6	13	33.0	34	86.4
3/4	19	1.9	14	35.6	35	88.9
7/8	22	2.2	15	38.1	36	91.4
1	25	2.5	16	40.6	37	94.0
1 1/4	32	3.2	17	43.2	38	96.5
1 1/2	38	3.8	18	45.7	39	99.1
1 3/4	44	4.4	19	48.3	40	101.6
2	51	5.1	20	50.8	41	104.1
2 1/2	64	6.4	21	53.3	42	106.7
3	76	7.6	22	55.9	43	109.2
3 1/2	89	8.9	23	58.4	44	111.8
4	102	10.2	24	61.0	45	114.3
4 1/2	114	11.4	25	63.5	46	116.8
5	127	12.7	26	66.0	47	119.4
6	152	15.2	27	68.6	48	121.9
7	178	17.8	28	71.1	49	124.5
8	203	20.3	29	73.7	50	127.0

Index